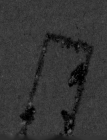

THE BICYCLE—
THAT CURIOUS INVENTION

THE BICYCLE—
THAT CURIOUS
INVENTION

by

Stephen and Sybil Leek

THOMAS NELSON INC., PUBLISHERS
NASHVILLE   /   NEW YORK

Copyright © 1973 by Stephen and Sybil Leek

All rights reserved under International and Pan-American Conventions. Published by Thomas Nelson Inc., Publishers, Nashville, Tennessee, and simultaneously in Don Mills, Ontario, by Thomas Nelson & Sons (Canada) Limited. Manufactured in the United States of America.

Second Printing

Library of Congress Cataloging in Publication Data

Leek, Stephen.
    The bicycle—that curious invention.

    SUMMARY: Traces the invention and development of the bicycle, describes some unusual models, and discusses its use in peace and war.
    1. Bicycles and tricycles—History—Juvenile literature. [1. Bicycles and bicycling] I. Leek, Sybil, joint author. II. Title.
TL410.L35   388.34'72
ISBN 0-8407-6260-7   73-14878

Acknowledgments

We would like to acknowledge the cooperation received from companies and individuals on both sides of the Atlantic. We found tremendous enthusiasm for our book, and made many new friends as we went about our research work. Pedal-power people are surely among the kindest in the world. They gave us hospitality, inspiration, information, and photographs—in addition to a strangely intangible feeling that we were among worthy descendants of those early designers and enthusiasts who brought the bicycle through the industrial revolution and through several wars right into the space age of Aquarius.

Thank you all—Dunlop Rubber Co. Ltd.; Raleigh Industries Ltd.; The Cyclists Touring Club of Great Britain; The Glasgow Museum of Transport, Scotland; Nicholas Hare of Thatchway Garage, Littlehampton, England; The Science Museum, London, England; Arnold, Schwinn & Co. of the U.S.A.; Bicycle World of Satellite Beach, Florida; British Cycling Bureau; Brevard Safety Council; *Popular Science; Modern Living;* Certificate Marketing Co.; *Orlando Sentinel-Star;* Missileland Wheels of Cocoa, Florida; Bob Jackson; Martin Caidin; Julian Leek; Rita Nunely; Jack Taylor; Lord Montagu of Beaulieu; and The Montagu Motor Museum. And the hundreds of cyclists we have met on the roads of Europe and the United States of America.

Stephen Leek
Sybil Leek

This book is dedicated
to the designers of bicycles:
past, present, and future.

Contents

"There has not been a more civilizing invention in the memory of the present generation than the invention of the bicycle, open to all classes, enjoyed by both sexes and by all ages."

—LORD BALFOUR

CHAPTER ONE

THAT CURIOUS
INVENTION

"Father! Quick, quick . . . come out here . . . quick!"

"What is it, Hans? This horseshoe is just hot enough for . . . *Mein Gott!* I don't believe my eyes!"

"It's the mad Baron, isn't it? Baron von Drais?"

"He must be *verrückt*. . . . Now he is really crazy! The Baron thinks he is a horse this time, no doubt."

"He's sweating like one—look how red his face is!"

"Someone should stop him before he hurts himself. Only an idiot would hitch a saddle to two carriage wheels and then try to run when he's sitting down!"

Indeed, it was the highlight of the year 1816 for the blacksmith and his son and all the other people who lived in the peaceful German town of Karlsruhe. The crazy Baron, who had quite a reputation for inventing the most useless gadgets, was at it again. But his latest contraption was just too much!

Yes, the saddle really was connected between two small carriage wheels. But the wheels were not side by side, as any normal person would have arranged them. Instead, one had been placed in front of the other, like two horses in tandem, and any fool could see that it was nearly impossible to balance the thing. The Baron looked as if he were riding a rail!

He would run for a bit, then raise his feet off the ground, swaying precariously with both hands gripping some sort of handle. He was actually trying to make the front wheel turn either to the right or the left.

"What have you got there, Herr Baron?" called one old resident of Karlsruhe. "Do you want to kill yourself?"

"Worse still, he is likely to kill *us!*" shouted the blacksmith as he moved back to the safety of a wall. The Baron was making the dust swirl in the narrow street, causing chaos among people who were going about their business.

"It's my new invention, the Drais *Lauf-Maschine!*" the Baron yelled. He weaved his way dangerously around the small crowd that had gathered while all the dogs in the neighborhood barked and yelped at the sight of the monstrous invention. The impact on the populace of Karlsruhe was as if some being from outer space had invaded their community. It was impossible for them to realize that they were witnessing the birth of a vehicle that was going to revolutionize transport.

And so the bicycle was born among derisive calls and yelping dogs—yet with some indulgence to the mad Baron who, after all, was a member of the community. While the *Lauf-Maschine* bore little resemblance to the eight-hundred-dollar titanium bicycles of the 1970's, the basic principle remains the same. If you will look in a modern dictionary for the word *bicycle,* the definition you will find there will fit not only today's ten-speed racers but also the Baron's original *Lauf-Maschine* of 1816:

> bicycle, bī'sik•al, *n.* (L. prefix *bi,* two, and Gr. *kyklos,*
> a circle or wheel.) A vehicle consisting of two wheels,
> one behind the other, connected by a light frame

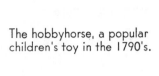

The hobbyhorse, a popular children's toy in the 1790's.

The hobbyhorse begins to look like a bicycle.

The *Lauf-Maschine* of Baron von Drais, 1818.

carrying a seat, the vehicle being propelled by the
feet of the rider. . . .

If it had not been for that strange ride along the narrow
street in Karlsruhe in 1816, it is doubtful if Baron von Drais
Sauerbronn would have been remembered as anything more
than a local eccentric. Despite his title, the Baron was chief
forester for the Duke of Baden, and one of his official duties
was to patrol the hundreds of acres of forest that were part of
the Duke's domain. The Baron was not very fond of his job.
More than anything else, he liked to spend his time using his
imagination and creativity to invent mechanical gadgets. He
spent all his money on his inventions, and rumor in the town
said that he was too poor to own a horse. It was no doubt
this lack of transport which made him think of inventing
something that might enable him to travel more easily on the
forest paths. His Drais *Lauf-Maschine* was meant to be the
answer to sore feet and tired legs, but it was crudely constructed and a lot of physical energy was still necessary to
make the vehicle move. No wonder the townsfolk of Karlsruhe
viewed it with indulgent contempt; they had seen too many
of the Baron's previous useless inventions, which had lived
for a day and then were cast aside to rust around his house.
What they could not foresee was that the Baron, with all his
reputation for being a mad eccentric, was for the first time in
his life on to something that could be developed into a useful
means of transport.

The basic construction of the Drais *Lauf-Maschine,* later
called the Draisine, was very simple. It consisted of a backbone of wood attached to two carriage wheels in tandem. To
this the Baron added a saddle and a back rest at the dip of
the backbone, plus a contraption like a tiller for steering. The
hubs of the wheels were connected to the wooden backbone
by two V-shaped uprights. To provide propulsion, the Baron
sat on the saddle and pushed hard with his feet to make the

curious invention move. In this way he could get up speed and then rest his legs for a few minutes, leaning against the back rest. Given plenty of space on the road—that is, when he was not impeded by onlookers and their attendant noisy dogs —he could make running movements with his legs and gather speed quite rapidly. The invention served the purpose of allowing him to move more quickly than he would normally walk, but if he hoped to save his legs from tiredness, then the Baron had made a mistake, for the machine needed a lot of physical effort to maintain mobility. It was certainly not a vehicle for all roads and purposes, and for it to be effective the Baron needed long stretches of open road and a lot of downhill coasting.

Naturally the people of Karlsruhe were not prepared to give him the freedom of their streets for his new contraption, and they soon sought legal measures to restrict him from riding around the town. It was no new thing for the Baron to have the citizenry up in arms against him; that is a problem many inventors have to put up with. No one really loves a new invention in its early stages; it is always inconvenient to less imaginative minds. People always find it easier to dismiss imagination and creativity by saying the inventor is mad. The miracle is that derision and lack of personal popularity never stop the truly dedicated inventor; he has a compulsion to go on.

Such was the case with Baron von Drais. He was genial by nature and loved children, who were far more interested in his vehicle than their parents were. So he went happily about his business, kicking away on the roads and laughing as he coasted along.

It is highly improbable that he saw himself in the guise of a man with a mission to fulfill; he could not dream that his curious invention would be the ancestor of the modern vehicle which we call the bicycle. Like most inventors, he was to know controversy, which grew as the news of his Draisine spread. There were others who felt they had a prior claim. National dignity became an issue, for when the French heard about the Baron and his Draisine, they were furious. They claimed that the Chevalier de Sivrac had produced a similar machine some twenty-six years before the Baron had startled the townsfolk of Karlsruhe. To a certain extent the French were right, but even so, similar forms of transport had been known a hundred or more years before even the Chevalier de Sivrac was born.

Although the invention of the Chevalier de Sivrac was a predecessor of the Draisine, its only link with it was that it consisted of two wheels in tandem. The Baron had added a steering mechanism, and that made all the difference between a viable vehicle and one that was little more than a toy. The Baron's first impulse had been to make his vehicle maneuverable—an important point in the development of the bicycle into the form we know today.

Another French contender to the claim of being the parent of the bicycle was Nicéphore Niepce, who had indeed recognized the value of a two-wheeled vehicle that could be steered, but he was not successful in his claim.

Although the Baron was not supposed to be a good businessman, some instinct made him apply for protection of his Draisine. On January 12, 1818, he was granted the following order:

> We, by the grace of God, Duke of Baden, grand Duke of Zahringen, grant to Karl, Baron von Drais, for his invention of tread machine an invention patent for ten years' duration that no one can copy or have copied in the land of the Grand Duchy, or shall use this on public streets or places without first having settled with the inventor about it, and to have gotten proof of it from him.

In Paris, in the same year, Louis Dineur took out a patent for the Baron, referring to the machine as a velocipede, although it became colloquially known by the French as the Draisienne. The invention was introduced into England in 1819, where the name was anglicized to Draisine. Later even the Germans began to refer to the Baron's *Lauf-Maschine* as the Draisine, and this name is commonly used in history books. People date the modern bicycle from Baron von Drais's invention, mainly because he was smarter than people thought and was able to obtain a great deal of personal publicity through it.

It is possible that without the Baron's invention some great (and not-so-great) moments in history might never have happened. The Wright brothers, for instance, earned their living as owners of a bicycle repair shop in Dayton, Ohio, while they tinkered with the world's first flying machine. John Dos Passos, in his 1936 poem "The Campers at Kitty Hawk" asserts that Wilbur and Orville's "homemade contraption" was "gummed together with Arnstein's bicycle cement."

"Look, Ma, no hands!"—to be followed by "Look, Ma, no teeth!"—would never have invaded Americanese were it not for the bike. There would be nothing for the movie's *Bicycle Thief* to steal. Eight hundred million Chinese would be without transportation. And Harry Dacre would never have penned his immortal tribute to "Daisy Bell" in 1892:

> I can't afford a carriage,
> But you'll look sweet upon the seat
> Of a bicycle built for two!

Bicycles built for two were also around in Baron von Drais's day. Engravings of the period show elegantly gowned and coiffured ladies perched on an extra seat behind the hard-kicking "driver." Remember, the Baron's "bike" had no pedals,

The velocipede invented by Dr. J. Richard, c. 1819.

no chain drive, and, worst of all, no brakes! Going down a hill meant losing the leather soles of your shoes. That gave the cobblers a booming business, but made the blacksmiths rise up in arms. In their opinion, sensible men should be wearing out their horses' shoes, not their own!

The blacksmiths were right in a way, for few "sensible" men respond to inventive genius. The *Lauf-Maschine* was the plaything of the dandies—rakish fops who loved to show off. And, sure enough, the *Lauf-Maschine* became known as the "dandy horse," which was more an expression of ridicule than affection. Therefore, despite the fact that *Ackermann's Magazine*, one of the most famous publications of its time, praised the

Baron's invention in its February 1819 issue in an article entitled "A Curious Invention," the Drais *Lauf-Maschine* eventually died out because of public disinterest.

However, the Baron's idea did not die out, and in 1891 a monument was erected to his name in his native city of Karlsruhe. It was a monument to a man who had been derided in his lifetime, and penalized by local laws, but whose name had survived to leave his mark in history. The *Court Journal* of May 2, 1891, printed this notice:

> On Sunday last, Karlsruhe, the native city of Karl von Drais, Baron of Sauerbronn, discharged her debt of honor to the inventor of the bicycle. Baron von Drais was born in 1785. Originally a forester, he devoted most of his time to inventions, which swallowed the whole of his fortune and procured for him the nickname "Professor of Mechanics." Although today the bicycle is in universal use, scarcely anything is known of the inventor, who gave the new locomotor the name "Draisine." It has been decided to erect a handsome monument over the grave of the inventor, the expense of which will be exclusively borne by bicyclists, thereby carrying his name down to the sportsmen of posterity.

Today we refer to the Baron von Drais as the "father of the bicycle." Most of his fellow townspeople lived and died making shoes for horses, working as tailors, or doing everyday chores. They had the reputation of being sane, orderly people. But no one erected any statues to them. In the end the mad Baron had the last laugh over the blacksmith and his son, who saw only the ludicrous elements in that curious invention which was to become the bicycle.

CHAPTER TWO

WHO PUT THE "BI" IN BICYCLE?

The idea that human muscular effort might be applied to the propulsion of a vehicle is a very old one. Over two thousand years ago horse-drawn chariots sped along the roads in ancient Egypt and Rome, making great demands on the skill of the men driving them. But other men in canoes raced in the rivers —their own propulsion creating the energy needed to get from one place to another. Why couldn't this man power be utilized on land?

In India, maharajahs were transported from place to place in sedan chairs carried upon the shoulders of slaves. Logically, the princes could move only as fast as their slaves could walk or run. The problem was speed. Everyone knew that an object going down a hill could move faster than one going up. Yet running slaves can run only so fast.

The answer to the problem lay in the wheel. A stained-glass window in an English church dating back to 1642 depicts a boy musician seated on a two-wheeled contraption very much like a bicycle. Bas-reliefs of Egypt and Babylon and frescoes in Pompeii depict a crude vehicle not unlike today's go-carts,

Stained-glass window in Stoke Poges Church, England, 1642.
Note boy musician riding a bicyclelike contraption.

beloved of children everywhere. This device supported the
body while the feet of the passenger provided the motive
power—the basic and original principle of the bicycle, except
that the ancient go-carts had four wheels. True, the power
needed to propel a bicycle is now applied differently, and
through the ages numerous mechanical aids have been added
to take the strain off the feet, but we should never forget that
the simple go-cart does, indeed, have a link with the bicycle.

Over the centuries, variations on four-wheeled, human-
propelled vehicles multiplied like flies in a marmalade pot.
Man had the nucleus of an idea. Toward the end of the Middle
Ages, Giovanni Fontana, the rector of the Faculty of Arts at
Padua in Italy, designed a machine that moved when the
rider pulled "an endless rope running around a pulley that
actuated the rear wheels through gearing." A couple of hundred years later, several of these crude carriages were actually
built in Nuremberg by Johannes Hautsch.

There is a description of an interesting pedal-operated carriage invented in 1696 by Dr. Elie Richard of La Rochelle, France. In this "quadricycle," the passenger sat in front under a circular awning and steered by means of a complicated array of cords attached to a swiveling front axle. Behind him, a footman (in the literal sense of the word) did all the hard work of propelling the carriage by pedaling two treadles, interconnected so that as one rose, the other fell. These treadles turned the rear axle by the use of gears and ratchet mechanisms. Quadricycles continued to be built for over a hundred

A quadricycle was a good way to see the countryside in the eighteenth century. The vehicle was propelled by the footman at the back, who pedaled two interconnected treadles.

and fifty years, but they were used mainly by wealthy eccentrics.

One of the first recorded notices of a kind of bicycle being used was in 1789, when a two-wheeled "phaeton" was seen in London. It was propelled by the feet of its rider without the aid of a footman or any other person. Various other designs

There was not much traffic on the road when this gentleman found fun riding his "curious invention."

were invented between then and 1791, when the *Célerifère* first appeared in France. Interestingly, this machine, later called the *Vélocifère*, was created from a popular toy, the hobbyhorse.

The Chevalier de Sivrac, who developed the *Célerifère*, thought it would be great fun to replace the hobbyhorse's rockers with wheels. Soon the body of the horse became that of a lion or of other animals—even serpents! Because the *Célerifère* was two-wheeled and the wheels were in tandem, the Chevalier's supporters claim today that he should be regarded as the true father of the bicycle. Experts point out, however, that the *Célerifère* could not be steered. Baron von Drais's *Lauf-Maschine* was steerable because the front wheel was pivoted on the frame—and this maneuverability made it practical.

The man who copied and promoted the *Lauf-Maschine*, or Draisine, in Britain was a London coachmaker, Denis Johnson, who in 1819 lived in Long Acre, a rural suburb of London. Johnson called his Draisine a Pedestrian Curricle, and he sold it for eight or ten guineas (about twenty-five dollars), which was as much as the average Londoner earned in a year! Clearly the device was for the wealthy only.

Johnson also set up a riding school for those who wished to become proficient in the management of the Pedestrian Curricle. A contemporary commentator wrote, "A person who has made himself tolerably well acquainted with the management of one can, without difficulty, urge himself forward at the rate of eight, nine, or even ten miles an hour."

Johnson built hundreds of the machines, and even introduced a ladies' model. John Keats, the poet, characterized the device as the "nothing" of the day, and caricature artists found plenty of inspiration for their drawings.

Nevertheless, there were a few people who were thinking instead of laughing. London's *Ackermann's Magazine* described

Macmillan's bicycle, the first two-wheeler with pedals, 1838.

the motivating principle of the Draisine as "being akin to the art of skating." The writer conjectured that such a vehicle could be put to good use by messengers and could, with the addition of saddle pouches, hold merchandise or the personal belongings of the rider. It must have been a cumbersome machine because it weighed fifty pounds and made great demands on the strength and stamina of the rider. The vehicle's potential had attracted the attention of men in three countries, and soon other inventive minds were seeking ways to improve on its appearance and performance.

The methodical approach to patenting the *Lauf-Maschine* and the many intrepid demonstrations of it started a spate of inventions designed to bring the bicycle into our own age as an almost perfect form of transport. However, it took time for these first inventions to get under way and not much real improvement was made until 1839. Then a Scottish blacksmith called Kirkpatric Macmillan invented the first pedal-operated bicycle. Like the *Vélocifère*, this vehicle had a wooden frame and wooden wheels with iron bands, but an important development was its wooden treadles, which drove cranks on the rear wheels by means of connecting rods. The machine had now become recognizable as an ancestor of the bicycles we ride today.

Macmillan rode his new vehicle with great pride, sometimes as far as fourteen miles in one day. He made a special niche for himself in history when, in 1842, he became the first man ever to get a ticket and to be fined for a bicycling offense. He knocked down a child and was fined five shillings (about one dollar). This accident occurred at the end of a grueling forty miles from Courthill to Glasgow, a journey that took him two days.

The first interest in bicycles waned slightly, and Macmillan's machine never became popular—although he must have had great fun in making those early rides on a machine that was his special brainchild. Today his original bicycle no longer exists, but a contemporary copied it and this machine may be seen in the Museum of Transport in Glasgow, Scotland. It was made by Gavin Dalzell in 1845 and employed all the main features of Macmillan's bicycle, such as the drive by means of treadles and rods to the cranks in the rear axle, plus the iron-rimmed wooden wheels. There were, of course, no brakes. For many years, people thought Dalzell was the inventor of the bicycle, mainly because it is his version that still exists and that has the distinction of being the oldest surviving pedal bicycle in the world. Another version of the Macmillan bicycle was made about 1860 by another compatriot called Thomas McCall. It had the additional refinement of a rear-wheel brake.

Meanwhile, Germany had been striving to produce its own version of the new wonder of manumotive vehicles. In 1852 a bicycle was built by Philip Fischer of Obendorf. He was a teacher at the Schweinfurt Technical School and used his bicycle to go to and from work. It was driven by pedals on the front wheel and, considering its pioneer status, was very well equipped, having a hand brake, a box over the rear wheel for luggage, a bell operated by a striker that was actuated by the spokes of one of the wheels, and, somewhat incongruously, a socket to hold a whip. The whip was probably used to discourage any stray dogs that Fischer might meet. Like Macmillan's, Fischer's invention seemed to have been constructed only for the delight and pleasure of its owner.

Inventive genius often runs in families, and it is worthy of mention that Friedrich Fischer, son of Philip, devised the automatic process for the production of steel balls, thereby making mass-produced ball bearings available for use on bicycles and other machinery. Some ten years after Fischer had constructed his bicycle, another German, Karl Kech, fitted pedals to the front wheels of a hobbyhorse, but his invention did not seem to lead to further developments in his native land.

In the same period, activity was going on in France, but many points are in doubt, including the question of who deserves the credit for the evolution of the French bicycle. In 1861, Pierre Michaux and his son Ernest, makers of baby carriages, started to fit cranks and pedals to a bicycle that they were repairing. They were helped by their mechanic, a man called Pierre Lallement, and some people are inclined to believe that he was responsible for the idea. Credulity is given to this belief by the fact that Pierre Lallement left his employers in a fit of temper and emigrated to the United States.

The Michaux family developed a machine that became known as the velocipede. They produced two machines in 1861 and 142 in 1862. By 1865 their annual output had grown to over 400. But Lallement beat them to full recognition by taking out in 1866 the first known patent on a bicycle. He

Ernest Michaux with his velocipede. His mechanic, Pierre Lalle-ment, brought the design into the United States.

joined forces for a while with James Carrol of Ausonia, Con-necticut, but their company was only moderately successful. Lallement then went to work for the Pope Manufacturing Company. Finally he returned to Paris to find that the Michaux family was well away in their own manufacturing business.

The Michaux-Lallement type of bicycle became affection-ately known as the boneshaker. For a few years, it enjoyed the attention of those dashing young men who come along in every generation to take on everything that is different and dangerous. At that time no one thought that a woman would ever ride a bicycle. It was a vehicle oriented to the image of masculinity, and certainly the boneshaker was not constructed to give much encouragement to ladies.

In the mid-nineteenth century most people were lucky if they ever traveled more than ten miles from their place of birth. Traveling then was a luxury, albeit an uncomfortable one, and was reserved for the wealthy. American and European designers and inventors accepted the boneshaker as a challenge to their ingenuity, for they realized that it was a form of transportation that almost everyone could afford and enjoy.

The British bicycle manufacturers were the first to take the lead in recognizing their product's huge potential. Rowley B. Turner, the Paris agent of the Coventry Sewing Machine Company, realized that the French manufacturers, dominated by

The velocipede, or boneshaker.
Courtesy Montagu Motor Museum, Beaulieu, Hants., England

A typical "penny-farthing" of 1869.

Courtesy Montague Motor Museum, Beaulieu, Hants., England

the Michaux family, could not satisfy the growing demand for bicycles. He persuaded his parent company to start building machines for export to France. In 1868 the company—now called Coventry Machinists Company—exported four hundred bicycles. But in 1870 the Franco-Prussian War closed down the French market, and the English firm, now geared to high production, was compelled to find outlets for its bicycles in its native land.

War also reduced the manufacture of French bicycles, and

The Phantom, 1869.

France never fully recovered from the setback. Thus Britain was left free to become the center of the world's bicycle manufacturing industry.

Coventry had a head start on other areas of Britain because it already had plants that could produce any number of machines, and had a vast army of designers always available. Their combined brains produced many new features on the boneshaker and the velocipede. Iron replaced wood for every part except the wheels, and rubber was used on them instead of iron bands. There were also refinements such as leg rests.

The public was ready for custom-made luxury machines, and the manufacturers were ready to meet these demands among other things. These luxury bicycles had ivory handle-bars and grips, ebony wheels, and backrests with springs. Anything that could add to the social status of the buyer and give him a special pride of ownership attracted new devotees to bicycling. The main interest, however, was in increased speed, which overcame even the interest in stability. The hobbyhorse had wheels of equal size, as did the early Michaux velocipedes, and they gradually became easier to propel as the weight was reduced.

The later velocipedes came out with front wheels of thirty-six inches in diameter and a thirty-inch rear wheel. This process of adding to the diameter of the brake wheel and re-ducing the rear one continued until the original boneshaker had become a reasonably elegant machine, with a high front wheel and a small back one.

At first they were known as "Ordinary" bicycles, but this name was changed to penny-farthing. The British love strange puns, and the new name was derived from the money of the day. Part of the currency of the realm was a very large, thick penny called a cartwheel, while one of the smallest coins was the farthing, in value worth a quarter of a penny. When a cartwheel penny was placed against a farthing, the difference in size was very noticeable and they seemed to resemble the large front wheel and the comparatively incongruous small back wheel of a bicycle.

A compromise between the old boneshaker and the Ordinary bicycle came between 1869 and 1872 when the machine's evolu-tion took a spectacular and revolutionary turn. This came about through the work of W. F. Reynolds and J. A. Mays, who produced a bicycle called the Phantom. The wheel sizes were similar to those of the velocipede, but the Phantom had an articulated (jointed) and triangulated frame constructed of light iron rods. The original wooden frame was discarded, but wooden wheels were still used for some time. The wheels had double wire spokes consisting of a double length of wire threaded through an eye on the rim of the wheel, then clamped to the hub, or center, of the wheel by means of flanges. Tension was achieved by moving the flanges apart. The suspension wheel had been invented and patented as early as 1802 by G. F. Bauer, and was often used during the first half of the nineteenth century for large water wheels. This was the first practical application of it to a bicycle. Perhaps the most novel feature of the Phantom, to our eyes, was that steering in later models was accomplished by means of the hinged frame instead of the usual pivoting front wheel.

CHAPTER THREE

MAINLY TRICYCLES

It is likely that the first tricycle was a hand-propelled machine constructed in the seventeenth century by Stephen Farffler, a cripple living in the German town of Altdorff. Presumably he constructed his machine to help him get around. Therefore, in addition to being the first known example of the tricycle, his machine was an early invalid carriage.

The advent of the hobbyhorse and later the Draisine increased interest in three-wheeled machines as well. In fact, at every stage in the evolution of the bicycle, someone was always around to make a three-wheeled version. Tricycles, however, were produced only on an individual basis from 1791 until 1870. Then interest in them increased.

There was a Ladies' Parisian tricycle that became popular in the 1860's and was in use for the next twenty years. It consisted of two rear wheels, driven by foot-operated rods and cranks, and a small front steering wheel, with a bucket seat located over the rear axle. This tricycle was fashionable at the English and German health resorts where ladies went to take the mineral waters. One version became known as the Bath chair, probably because Bath, in England, was one of the most fashionable of all the genteel health spas. Even today, it is

The Coventry Lever tricycle, 1876.
Courtesy Montague Motor Museum, Beaulieu, Hants., England

not uncommon to discover an old Bath chair hidden away in the stables or outhouses of an English country house. These early tricycles are in great demand by antique dealers.

The Ordinary bicycle of the mid 1870's was in many respects a better machine than its ancestor, but it had one disadvantage.

The huge size of the front wheel made it unstable and, as the demand for personal transport grew, many people felt they needed something easier and safer to ride than a bicycle. The answer was the tricycle, and from 1876 onward, three-wheeled machines were built in ever greater numbers.

Although Coventry in England became the world center of bicycle production and France made its special contribution by way of making accessories and gearing devices, the first really practical tricycle originated from neither of these countries but from Ireland. In 1876 William Blood took out a patent for a tricycle with a single rear driving wheel and twin steerable front wheels. The front wheels were much smaller than the rear one. Mounted on forks, they pivoted in a manner

The Coventry Rotary tricycle, 1876.

similar to the front wheel of a bicycle. Treadles and rods connected to cranks on the rear axle created the drive on the rear wheel.

The company of Carey Brothers of Dublin manufactured the first commercial tricycles, and their design became known as the Dublin tricycle. Then the Coventry company of Hillman and Herbert was licensed to produce the Dublin in England

This four-wheeled cycle of 1885 was prepelled by both riders.
Courtesy Montague Motor Museum, Beaulieu, Hants., England

and ultimately became its sole manufacturer. They had developed a machine of their own, but dropped it in favor of the Dublin design.

James Starley, whose name was well known in connection with two-wheeled machines, was also interested in producing some of the early tricycles. His tricycle was almost an accidental offshoot, a sort of by-product, of his work on bicycles. Realizing the potential of his two-wheeled Ariel as a machine light enough for ladies, he modified it expressly to meet their needs. The rear wheel was offset from the driving wheel and a padded seat placed over it. He extended the handlebars and replaced the pedals with a lever system. But the machine was still too difficult for a woman to ride until Starley modified it further by adding another wheel in front, turning it into a tricycle. It was manufactured by Haynes and Jefferies of Coventry, and was advertised in March 1877 as the Coventry Lever tricycle. Starley could always be relied upon to produce the ultimate vehicle to meet any need. The successful Coventry Lever tricycle had a distinctive design, with a large wheel on one side of the rider and two small, steerable wheels on the other. Later he replaced the lever action with chain drive, and in this form it became known as the Coventry Rotary, but the name was again changed to the Rudge Rotary. For the next ten years this was the most popular form of tricycle.

Starley then produced the Coventry Sociable, a four-wheeled machine that would take a passenger as well as the driver, with each person operating one driving wheel. Unfortunately, two people on a vehicle do not necessarily mean two minds with a single thought, and the Sociable was not as safe as the original three-wheeled vehicle. Starley finally dispensed with the small wheel and the Sociable went back to being a tricycle.

Starley liked to ride his own Sociable with his son William, and thus he conceived the idea of using differential gears to equalize the force they both exerted. Of course, the ideal arrangement for two people on a tricycle is for them to weigh the same. However, William Starley weighed considerably more than his father, and the imbalance made steering difficult when each of them pedaled his own wheel. The idea of differential gears was not really original with the senior Starley. They were already in use in steam traction engines at that time, and there were known examples of their earlier application. However, Starley was the first man to apply it to a tricycle.

By 1877 a great many tricycles were being manufactured. In 1877 and 1878, fifty-seven patents for tricycles were granted. There was now a demand for three-wheeled vehicles, and a production pattern was established. The tricycle maintained this popularity until almost the end of the century.

One of the most popular types was the "open-fronted" tri-

The Cheylesmore-type bicycle of 1885.
Courtesy Montague Motor Museum, Beaulieu, Hants., England

cycle, with two large front wheels and a single small rear wheel. It was produced by several manufacturers, including Starley and his partner William Sutton. The open front had the advantage of preventing the rider from getting entangled in the machine in the event of a spill.

The Coventry Machinists Company produced a tricycle in 1877 that became the prototype for the same company's "Cheylesmore" design.

Doubleday and Humber patented a unique tricycle in 1878 that had several claims to notability. Viewed from the side, it resembled an Ordinary bicycle, but it had two large front driving wheels that were chain-driven and steered by means of the handlebars. The use of handlebars on tricycles was rare during this period, the usual guiding device being some form of stirrup-shaped hand grip with a rack-and-pinion mechanism. The saddle of the Humber design was mounted on the backbone, just as it was with the ordinary bicycle. Since the pedals pivoted with the front wheels, the rider could steer this tricycle by using his feet.

Humber tricycles of 1878 were used for racing, but were not entirely successful in this field, as they had a tendency to swerve. The Devon tricycle, one of the first double-drive machines of this type, succeeded in overcoming the lack of adhesion prevalent in the single-drive types.

The omnicycle, patented by T. Butler in 1879, was similar to the Starley Royal Salvo, but it had a mechanism that varied the speed at which it could be driven. This mechanism, used on hills and bad roads, consisted of several hand-adjusted circles reciprocated by leather straps attached to the pedal stirrups. It was cumbersome and hard to manipulate, but interest in pedal vehicles was high, and enthusiasts would try anything once. Various designs were produced by W. H. J. Grout, who made a geared tricycle. It was a tremendous period for designers, who were always conscious that every vehicle

Gibbons' pentacycle, affectionately called The Hen and Chickens, was invented to help the post office deliver parcels.

produced was merely a forerunner to even better ones. The Excelsior One-Two-Three of 1879 was a rear-steered tricycle with three wheels of different sizes, the single chain drive being taken to the largest wheel.

Innovations followed year after year, but weight was always the bugbear. A ladies' "light" tricycle of about 1880 weighed about a hundred and ten pounds. It also needed an Amazon type to venture onto it. Technical developments and, in particular, the interest in racing, which demanded lighter ma-

A Humber tricycle of 1885.

Courtesy Montagu Motor Museum, Beaulieu, Hants., England

The Quadrant tricycle, made by Lloyd Brothers of Birmingham, England, 1882.

chines, eventually reduced the weight so that in 1882 it was possible to produce a racing tricycle. It was still more cumbersome than the bicycle, however. The main advantage of tricycles was safety, because the addition of the third wheel made them easier to balance.

The tricycle can really be said to have made its special mark in transport history in 1881, when it made its debut as a commercial vehicle. The first post office contract for parcel-carrying tricycles was given to Bayliss-Thomas Company of Coventry.

Britain's General Post Office established a precedent in using man-powered vehicles as part of its regular business life, and other companies and tradesmen began to use tricycles to speed up their delivery services. The commercial tricycle outlasted the purely passenger-carrying vehicles. In many parts of the world today, even in New York City, small tradesmen, such as the local grocer or butcher, still use tricycles for making deliveries.

The final form of the tricycle was introduced in 1881 by the Leicester Tricycle Company. Like the Humber, it had handlebar control, but the two parallel wheels were now placed in the back, with a single wheel in the front. While this layout of wheels was not entirely new, the Leicester tricycle was the first of this type to have indirect handlebar steering. The Humber also had handlebar steering, but it had two wheels in the front. Then a new Humber tricycle appeared on the market and became the first machine to have direct handlebar control of a single front steerable wheel. At first it was known as the Humber Automatic Steerer, but in its final form it was called the Humber Cripper after being ridden with great success in competitions by a rider named Robert Cripps.

About 1882 a new design appeared called the Quadrant; it was devised from patents obtained by W. J. Lloyd, and was manufactured by Lloyd Brothers of Birmingham, England. The axle of the steered wheels had rollers on its ends, which ran on curved bearing plates, or quadrants. This method of guiding the steering wheel took the place of conventional steering and was first applied to a vehicle with a steerable wheel at the rear. Before long, the position was altered to the front, and this form of the Quadrant enjoyed great popularity. By having a much larger steerable wheel than other tricycles, the Quadrant made a significant step toward the machine of today, with all three wheels of equal size.

Between 1880 and 1890 no one could complain about a lack

of choice if his inclination was directed toward a tricycle rather than a bicycle. At some of the trade shows, the tricycles outnumbered the bicycles, and there was a consistent interest in the two-seater machines. All the world, it seemed, liked to have company when riding. Both tandem and side-by-side

A German tricycle based on an American design.

The Humber tricycle owned by King Edward VII, 1907.
Courtesy Montagu Motor Museum, Beaulieu, Hants., England

seating arrangements had their devotees. If variety was thought to be the spice of life, then the numerous designs of tricycles supplied enough for everyone. But despite the random variations, there was a definite trend toward tricycles with two rear wheels and a single steerable front wheel, directly controlled by handlebars, and all of them of an equal size. By 1886 some companies were producing vehicles with three twenty-eight-inch wheels.

In 1888 Singer also came out with a version of this type of tricycle, incorporating into it all the features of the early "safety" bicycle frame. It also used the inclined steering head and curved front fork, which aligned the steering axis with the point of contact of the front tire with the ground.

Marriott and Cooper brought out the Olympia, a tandem tricycle that proved to be popular for touring and racing. The later versions were fitted with pneumatic tires. It was a compact machine with a short wheelbase, two front steering wheels, and its second seat located over the front axle. The two sets of pedals drove the single rear wheel by chains.

The older designs were not immediately superseded and continued to be produced for many years, but each year brought further evidence that the public preferred three wheels of equal size, two of them at the back, to the heavier, less stable, two-wheels-at-the-front models.

A disadvantage of direct steering with the reduction in the size of the driving wheels was that the rider suffered from a lot of vibration caused mainly by the state of the roads. Although the pneumatic tire was lurking in the wings ready to make its appearance, there was still time for tricycles with sprung frames to make a brief show. Some desultory attempts to provide springing had been made from time to time since 1869, but not until 1885 could this type of frame be considered satisfactory.

The pneumatic tire provided the answer to cutting down vibration, and by 1890 it was a regular feature in tricycles. By that time, however, it was too late for the tricycle to gain distinction over the bicycle. By 1892 there was a noticeable decline in the popularity of the tricycle because of the rapid improvement in the safety bicycle, which culminated in the application and acceptance of the pneumatic tire.

The Psycho tricycle was produced in 1895, and some expense was incurred in trying to promote it as the "tricycle for gentlemen." It had a diamond frame and was similar to the safety bicycles of the day, except for its three wheels of the same size—28 inches, with a 1¾-inch tread.

But the idea of three wheels as a means of stability was a practical one, and the memory of the tricycle, one-time rival to the bicycle, lingered on when miniature toy cycles were produced in vast numbers for children. Remember how the hobbyhorse started from a children's toy? A full swing of the pendulum brought the tricycle back to where everything started, and the three-wheeled cycle has been one of the most memorable experiences in many a child's life, helping to develop a taste for freedom that only the man-powered vehicle can give.

In the United States, tricycles for adults never really reached the degree of popularity that they did in Europe, although a few examples were seen around Boston and Washington. But America took the bicycle to its heart in no uncertain manner, for then, as now, the current craze in anything was geared to the whims of youth. Tricycles were somehow associated with elderly people, and there never was the devil-may-care attitude connected with them as there was with the bicycle.

The bicycle appealed to the spirit of eternal youth with its need for personal freedom. One can hardly visualize some dashing young "blood" scorching down a cycleway on a tricycle! The image simply did not fit in with the bright, innovative spirit of the Gay Nineties.

The tricycle died an early death in the United States because it could never achieve the éclat of the bicycle—yet by a strange paradox, the United States has probably manufactured more children's tricycles than any other country in the world.

CHAPTER FOUR

THE BICYCLE TAKES OVER

James Starley was to become known as the "father of the bicycle industry," and in 1870 he patented his "ribbon" wheel, using narrow brass ribbons for spokes. The bicycle was now ready to move into the world of big business and was to make Coventry as famous for bicycles as for Lady Godiva.

Starley formed a company in St. John's Street, Coventry, but, seeing the huge potential for commercial bicycles, he allowed his designs to be made under license by Haynes and Jefferies. In comparison to earlier bicycles, Starley's Ariel was a compact, almost streamlined, machine with a large front wheel and a small back one of elegant proportions, with the saddle situated close to the handlebars. One of the most important innovations was the use of a speed-gear, which Starley also invented. This enabled the front wheel to revolve at twice the speed of the crank spindle. It also made it possible for the rider to travel at a higher speed with much less strain on the body. In 1873 a Mr. James Moore rode at the unbelievable speed of fourteen and a half miles an hour and created a record for the age on his Starley-designed Ariel.

Bicycle racing made manufacturers try to produce stronger machines that weighed less and were capable of more and more speed. The boneshaker and the ordinary bicycle brought

James Starley's Ariel, commonly called the penny-farthing, 1871.

into being the first long-distance touring events and then bicycle clubs. One of the earliest of these, and the first to survive for any length of time, was the London-based Pickwick Cycling Club, founded in 1870. All over England, cycling clubs started to spring up. In 1878 the Bicycle Touring Club was formed, and it remains in existence today.

Yet the bicycle was still not perfect because the suspension wheel with its tension tightening of the spokes did not allow all of them to be adjusted simultaneously. The introduction of the nipple-type adjustment was brought about by an invention of W. H. J. Grout. It became available in a variety of sizes;

typical dimensions for the front and back wheels were 48 inches and 24½ inches, respectively. Machines ultimately became available with front wheels ranging from 60 inches to 41 inches. Grout's tension gadget made for a more serviceable machine, and this was capably demonstrated in June 1873 when four machines were ridden from London to John o'Groats, the most remote northern corner of Scotland, a distance of almost nine hundred miles. It dispelled the popular idea that the bicycle was for short-term journeys only. This feat proved the reliability of the machines as well as the stamina of the riders.

After that, the Ordinary bicycle developed rapidly and

The Cyclists Club of Great Britain arrive at the Inn at Potters Bar. The historic run of old-time cyclists on the Great North Road represented the boneshaker (1870), the Ordinary "penny-farthing" (1879), the tandem (1884), and the Sociable (1889).

Courtesy Cyclists Club of Great Britain

purchasers were able to have the choice of a number of designs at prices ranging from fourteen to fifty dollars. The early Ordinaries, like the boneshaker, employed solid frames, but next came frames made with hollow sections of metal. This practice was quickly adopted by the major bicycle manufacturers because lighter frames made it possible to go faster.

Although the Ordinary bicycles became popular, even the lowest-priced ones were too expensive for most people, who were earning pennies per day instead of dollars. And even with the new technical developments, bicycles were not easy

In 1880, many boys like Johnny Dunlop were riding bicycles.

to ride, so their use was mainly restricted to energetic young men.

In those days, elderly people were more conservative when it came to traveling. Even among the young, accidents were common events, with cyclists competing with other means of transportation on less-than-satisfactory roads. Instability was a key factor when bicycle and rider came together, providing fuel for people who considered that anything progressive and different must be bad. The lack of stability was the result of the distance of the rider from the ground and the bicycle's poor balance. His perch was precarious and when he fell off, it was quite a long way down. Accidents and broken limbs were part of the price paid by cyclists. The lack of lateral stability was bad enough, but it was the fore-and-aft stability that was especially deficient, making an involuntary descent over the handlebars a frequent occurrence, with the inevitable result of injury to the rider. It is likely that parents in those days threw up their hands in horror when their offspring bought a bicycle. The daring motorcyclists of today are only acting out a scene that has been played before.

Naturally, designers were aware of these defects and sought to overcome them. They followed two lines of thought simultaneously. There were designers who struggled to modify the existing machines and a new breed of inventor who foresaw that a radically different machine was the only answer.

A notable variation of the Ordinary bicycle was the Singer Xtraordinary, which appeared in 1878. This machine's front steering head was in line with the point of contact of the wheel and the ground, an important principle, which was to be universally adopted. It improved controllability by allowing the rider to be seated farther back, thus reducing the chance that his body would fly over the handlebars, a feat called nose diving, and a ripe subject for cartoonists. But because, in the rear seating position, the pedals in the front

The Singer Xtraordinary, 1878.

axle could not be used in their normal position, a system of linkages was employed.

Similar in principle to the Xtraordinary was the Facile bicycle patented by John Beale. In this machine, the front wheel was reduced from sixty to forty-eight inches. The rider sat well back and the pedals were connected to cranks on the front axle by means of a system of links. The Xtraordinary and the Facile provided a partial solution to the problems of the Ordinary bicycle. Time and the inspiration of man's inventive mind would supply further solutions, leading to better and safer bicycles.

Other manufacturers saw that Beale was on the right path and they continued to reduce the front wheel and, at the same time, to use some form of gearing so that the wheel turned faster than the pedals. A new design, introduced in 1884 and manufactured by Hillman, Herbert and Cooper, was called the Kangaroo. The driving wheel was only thirty-six inches in diameter and it was driven by chains moving at a higher speed than the pedals. A geared-up version of the Facile, using sun-and-planet gearing, appeared in 1888, but John Beale's machine had the advantage of weighing only thirty-two pounds while the other one weighed nearly fifty pounds.

From 1885 onward the new look in bicycles gained in popularity. The old-school inventors began to realize it was no use simply trying to modify the Ordinary bicycle, and decided to go along with the new school of designers. As machines with a geared-up chain drive to the rear wheel were produced in constantly growing numbers, the life of the Ordinary bicycle and the types derived from it came to an end.

By now the bicycle had become increasingly popular among all classes of people. They had tasted the joys of personal mobility and liked it. The bicycle, once the butt of derisive jokes, was still a popular theme among cartoonists, but now the subject was touched upon with warmth and fun rather than with jeering disapproval or grim warnings of dire things happening to those who rode the "curious invention."

Speed was gradually becoming aligned with safety, and they became the two key words associated with the next step in the development of the bicycle.

The term "safety" bicycle was once applied to any machine designed to be less dangerous than the high-front-wheeled Ordinary. For example, the Singer Xtraordinary and the

Kangaroo were first called safety bicycles. Gradually, as new designs appeared in increasing numbers, always aiming at increased stability on two wheels by reduction of the huge front wheel, the safety bicycle description was reserved for a specially constructed machine in which the rear wheel was driven, usually by a chain.

The origin of what was ultimately to become the safety bicycle is attributed to H. J. Lawson, but many of the designs that were ultimately brought to a state of perfection in the evolution of the bicycle always seem to go back beyond the names we accept.

For instance, a French clockmaker, André Guilmet, is thought to have produced a machine of this type in 1869, but it lay forgotten in a loft for many years due to the Franco-Prussian War. In the same year F. W. Shearing designed a safety machine that was illustrated in the *English Mechanic* magazine, but it was neither patented nor built. Thomas Shergold of Gloucester, England, made a safety bicycle and rode it himself about 1876. This machine can be seen in the Science Museum in London. It had nearly equal-sized wheels —twenty-nine inches in diameter at the front and thirty-two inches in the rear.

A year after Shergold, in 1877, a Monsieur Rousseau of Marseilles, France, was known to be riding a safety bicycle of his own construction, with a chain drive to the front wheel.

When we talk about a man who was the "father of the safety bicycle" or even the "father of the cycle," we always seem to be talking about the men who employed successful business methods to commercialize bicycles, and forget those who paved the way.

Macmillan of Scotland and Shergold of Gloucester made bicycles for their own use and pleasure, but it took a Singer, Haynes, Mays, or Reynolds to manufacture and sell large numbers of Ordinary bicycles. The same thing happened to

John Beale's Facile, 1878.

the safety bicycle. Guilmet, Shearing, and Shergold were adventurous men who were not mainly concerned with business, so the scene was left wide open for H. J. Lawson to produce the first commercial safety bicycle. This he did in 1879, and he called it the Bicyclette. It was his third attempt to design and produce a safety bicycle with commercial potential, and it was an important step in the solution of the rear-drive bicycle.

Lawson used the cross frame in which a single-member backbone joined a vertical forked support holding the pedal spindle and chain sprocket. A handlebar, connected by means of a coupling rod, gave more effective steering, and the saddle was placed well back to the rear of the frame.

Lawson did not realize that his design was revolutionary, and he made no immediate attempt to have it put into production. Then, in 1884, he approached the Birmingham Small

H. J. Lawson's safety bicycle, 1879.

Arms Company, known as BSA, and suggested that this firm market his Bicyclette. The company was set up to manufacture bicycles although it was mainly concerned with the production of small arms and engineering tools. They declined Lawsons' offer to manufacture, but agreed to make two prototypes for him.

Meanwhile, the company went ahead and designed and patented a safety bicycle of its own, making Lawson's efforts obsolete. BSA then happily sold some fifteen hundred safety bicycles for the equivalent of less than twenty-five dollars each! They called their product Safety. It had a thirty-two-inch chain-driven rear wheel, and a twenty-inch front wheel steered by means of a handlebar and two coupling rods.

Perhaps there was some consolation for H. J. Lawson in knowing he had inspired the BSA to go ahead with production. There is certainly no doubt that all other safety bicycles owe a debt of gratitude to this designer.

James K. Starley, nephew of the boneshaker designer of the same name, tried three times to produce a safety bicycle. His first design, in 1884, had a thirty-six-inch front wheel, coupling-rod steering, and a single backbone-type frame. In his second design, he followed a suggestion made by Stephen Golder, a Coventry competition cyclist. This resulted in a machine with direct steering and an adjustable saddle very similar to the one we know today.

Starley was in partnership with William Sutton, and they formed the Rover Company. From the complicated beginnings of the bicycle, this company was to grow into a giant in another field of transport—that of manufacturing automobiles. But before this event occurred in history, Starley had to make his name as the "father of the safety bicycle." His second design paved the way for this when, in September of 1885, the Rover Company organized several marathon cycle races. Obviously it was something of a publicity stunt, since it was restricted to machines made by Starley and Sutton, but this race certainly proved the stamina of their products as well as of the riders. The fifty-mile bicycle record was broken by Stephen Golder, who made the good time of three hours and five minutes for the course. The winner of the one-hundred-mile race was George Smith, who completed the course in seven hours, five minutes, and six seconds. Golder also competed in the one-hundred-mile race, but he managed to come in only at seventh position. Golder and Smith rode the new safety bicycles, while most of the other competitors pedaled Ordinary machines.

Starley's third design was developed from his first two prototypes and can be regarded as the production prototype of the present safety bicycle. It demonstrated in a convincing and practical manner the superiority of the safety arrangements of the frame design, the direct steering, and the low weight of thirty-seven pounds.

In the early days of the Rover Company, the main concern was to produce the ultimate in a safety bicycle, but the firm was quick to publicize the fact that the Starley-Sutton machines were so well built that they could climb hills easily and attain high speeds. This is not to say that the first safety machines combined all these attributes, for the company actually built two distinct models. One was very stable and safe, while the second was designed for speed, thus anticipating the modern racing cycle. Despite defects that are apparent today, Starley–Sutton machines were recognizable ancestors of the modern bicycle.

Gradually every manufacturer began to produce machines with wheels of equal size and a geared-up chain drive to the rear wheel. Each company added its own improvements to Starley's basic conception and, to a certain extent, his design was very close to Lawson's ill-fated Bicyclette. The big difference between Starley's machines and those produced by

The Singer safety bicycle, 1890.

others was that Starley preferred the triangulated diamond-type frame with straight tubes. There was, however, a considerable variety in frame designs. One manufacturer produced a frame like a cross, similar to the primitive form used by Lawson. For several years, a controversy raged about the benefits of the triangulated diamond frame and the cross one. Ultimately the diamond frame won out because of its greater stability, combined with tensile strength and lightness.

One of the most interesting types was an intermediate form called the Whippet, which had a sprung frame. It was patented in 1885 by O. MacCarthy and manufactured by Lindley and Biggs. Saddle, pedals, and handlebar were built on a rigid triangle, isolated from the main frame by a strong coil spring and a movable shackle in the steering mechanism. The

Whippet was popular for three years and broke a number of records during this period.

One notable cross-frame bicycle was the Ivel, produced in 1886 by Dan Albone, an agricultural engineer of Biggleswade, Bedfordshire. It broke a lot of records. Rudge and Singer also made cross-frame bicycles. The safety machine as it was produced and used in increasing numbers from 1880 to 1890 was a thoroughly serviceable vehicle, which had managed to avoid the vices of instability and heaviness. Members of the old school of bicyclists thought the new models were lacking in comfort because they had small wheels about twenty-eight to thirty inches in diameter and narrow, solid tires. The saddles were beginning to have springs in them, but there was still a lot of jarring with discomfort for the riders. That was caused as much by bad roads as by the designs of the bicycles.

Therefore, while strides had been made in achieving speed

A spring-frame bicycle made by Cooper, Kitchen & Co. about 1888.

Courtesy Art Gallery and Museum, Glasgow, Scotland

Johnny Dunlop on the tricycle to which his father, J. B. Dunlop, fitted his first experimental tires.

and safety, bicycles still needed to be made more comfortable for the cyclist. They did achieve a modicum of comfort with the placing of the saddle well back on the frame. However, a major event was about to happen that would be of supreme importance to all wheeled machines of the future, including the bicycle.

Amazingly enough, this world-shaking event was brought about by a Scottish veterinary surgeon called J. B. Dunlop. In 1888 he patented his version of the pneumatic tire.

Again we come into the area of mistakenly attributing the title "father of . . . " to J. B. Dunlop, for he was not the true "father of the pneumatic tire." As early as 1845 another Scot, R. W. Thomson, had already patented a pneumatic tire, which he thought would make coach and carriage riding more comfortable. Although the basic idea was never brought to fruition through manufacture, Dunlop really repatented an invention that had previously been patented. He was also smart enough to develop it. In so doing, he made a major contribution to the comfort of cyclists and, ultimately, automobile owners.

An inflatable hollow tire had been discussed frequently in the cycling press but was always dismissed as impractical. The genius of Dunlop was not in inventing the pneumatic tire but in realizing its potential and then going on to use his influence to get it manufactured. Thomson had found a compromise with his original idea and experimented for a short time with solid rubber tires on a steam traction engine, but with limited success. Dunlop went back to the basic principle of inflating a hollow rubber tire. At first his product added greatly to the cost of bicycles, but it quickly became popular as cyclists grew aware of the advantages of this more comfortable means of travel.

By 1892 the pneumatic tire was fitted to most cycles being produced. The sprung frames were gradually abandoned, and most makers brought out new models having frames with forks wide enough to take the pneumatic tires.

With the new style in tires fitted to the more acceptable diamond frame, we arrive at the more-or-less standard cycle of the present day. Naturally, more and more changes continued to be made, but they were largely aimed at improvements in details and the addition of accessories. At the same time, better production techniques allowed a less expensive machine to be produced, and rubber technology began to come into its own. Credit is due to Dunlop for his wisdom of seeing the potential of the pneumatic tire—but we should perhaps spare a thought for R. W. Thomson and give him credit for having the first creative vision and foresight to recognize that his invention must ultimately lead to comfort.

The patent obtained in 1888 by Dunlop started a new trend in bicycling, although it took two decades to really launch the pneumatic tire and make it an integral part of every cycle.

Another safety design of this period was the Crypto Geared Bantam. In effect, this machine was a small version of the Ordinary bicycle with a single central backbone. Its main contribution to the evolution of the bicycle was the Crypto epicyclic gear incorporated in the hub of the small front wheel. By means of this special gear, the pedals were geared up in relation to the driving wheel.

By 1890 the tendency was for the unorthodox experimental types to disappear through a gradual decline in use; the way was clear for the trend toward the diamond-frame safety bicycle. That year saw the production of the first modern form of diamond-frame bicycle, manufactured by the Humber Company. They made one specially constructed bicycle which they boasted had completed a journey of fifteen thousand miles across Europe, Asia, and America. The trip took four years, but was accomplished successfully with very few, and only minor, repairs having to be made on the frame. This Humber bicycle is preserved in the Science Museum in London, where the machine is exhibited complete with the make-shift binding of telegraph wire with which it completed the last fifteen hundred miles of the journey.

From the appearance of the boneshaker in 1860 to the Humber long-distance bicycle in 1890–1903, the weight of the bicycle had been reduced from between thirty-five and sixty pounds to from eighteen to forty pounds. Materials and manufacturing techniques could add further improvements because the main reduction of weight was due to the starkness of design and the cutting down of accessories.

The Osmond bicycle came out in 1896 and is another good example of a more fully developed form of the early diamond frame. It aroused interest because of its strong construction. It had twenty-eight-inch wheels with hollow steel rims.

The application of the roller-type driving chain, which appeared on the Osmond bicycle, increased the smoothness and efficiency of the drive to the rear wheel, and the earlier block-type chain gradually became obsolete. Attempts were also made to improve the drive by the use of other forms of transmission. As far back as 1882, the shaft drive and bevel gearing had been applied to propulsion by Samuel Miller; this was later used on the Columbia and Acatène bicycles. But the shaft drive for bicycle propulsion made little headway once the roller chain came into use.

The New Whippet of 1897 was another advanced machine for its time. It was fitted with such progressive features as a freewheel, a rim brake, and a four-speed gear. These were great advantages, giving the rider more control over his vehicle.

CHAPTER FIVE

FREAKS OF THE CYCLING WORLD

During the period in which the velocipede and Ordinary types of bicycles were being developed and adopted for use in many countries, there was also a movement to produce variations of man-powered vehicles. As early as 1868 several attempts had been made to produce a satisfactory single-wheeled bicycle called the monocycle, but it did not meet with much success. The monocycle evolved as a vehicle for circus performers to use in specialist acts. With its simple construction it is by far the easiest way to ensure a practically perfect distribution of wheel load. Its drawback is its instability—fore, aft, and laterally—but that, of course, is why it appeals to acrobats. Although the monocycle is unsuitable for the ordinary rider, an expert using one in the circus can amuse spectators with his difficult balancing feats. The helter-skelter antics of a small group of clowns on monocycles seem to intrigue audiences all over the world.

On a monocycle, the rider sits at or about the center of a large wheel, or else he sits astride a small wheel (or system of wheels) rolling within a larger one. He operates the single wheel by using hand cranks, his feet generally being supported

on rests or in stirrups. Sometimes the wheel is driven by cranks and pedals.

An early example of the monocycle, produced in the 1860's, was used primarily in the circus, but a "sociable" monocycle was made by Pearce in 1881. When the word "sociable" is used in cycle history, it means a system of side-by-side seating for two passengers. The Pearce sociable had two seats mounted on extensions of the wheel spindle, which had suitable handle-bars attached to it. Downward extensions supported the pedal spindle brackets. These spindles had chain sprockets mounted on them, which took the drive to the wheel.

The "dicycle" employs two wheels of equal diameter mounted parallel to one another on a common spindle. This type of bicycle first appeared in 1866. The model had two wheels, each ten feet in diameter, which ran freely on a common axle. The axle was formed with a cleft in the center in which the rider was supported by two T-shaped handles. He propelled the vehicle by thrusting at the ground with his feet, as with the primitive hobbyhorse type of bicycle. The dicycle was not popular when it came out, but was regarded as a novelty. The Birmingham Small Arms Company (BSA) designed one from a series of patents taken out by E. C. D. Otto between 1879 and 1881, and about a thousand models were produced. The Otto dicycle was fitted with a saddle and with pedal cranks that transmitted the effort of the driver to the two driving wheels by the use of pulleys and spring-loaded belts. Once the art of balancing on the dicycle was achieved, it was very maneuverable, but success depended on the skill of the rider plus his spirit of adventure. Man's sixth sense

Trick and comedy cycling, such as performed here by circus clown Slarri, never fails to amuse the crowds.

Courtesy Dennis Assinder

may be his sense of balance rather than a mysterious association with the occult.

The sociable style of riding enjoyed a brief vogue, but the idea of two cyclists riding one in front of the other was much more practical. This is the principle of the tandem. Sketches were made for two-rider machines as far back as 1819, but it is doubtful if anyone rode one until 1869.

Americans can always be relied upon to improve the ideas of others, and it was an American, H. T. Butler, who is regarded as the father of the tandem. When he was in the senior class at Harvard Law School, Butler was an enthusiastic

A tricycle made for two.

velocipede rider, and it occurred to him that a bicycle could move faster and with less effort if two people were mounted on it. He made a sketch and wrote a brief description of his idea, and sent them to Munn and Company, publishers of *Scientific American* magazine. But Butler's idea only remained on paper and his tandem was not put into production.

Then, many years later, J. Rucker decided to produce a vehicle that could be ridden by two people, one in front of the other. On May 9, 1884, Rucker obtained a patent for a very simple design. He simply took two high wheels from Ordinary bicycles and attached them together with a bar. Each rider was mounted above a wheel. It must have required a lot of courage and ingenuity to mount this tandem, much less ride it. The Kangaroo tandem of 1884 had counterbalanced pedals which made for a smoother ride, but the machine was still cumbersome and unstable. It was never a commercial success.

The tandem was developed to a greater potential across the Atlantic. In 1886 in England, Dan Albone and his partner, A. J. Wilson, were responsible for the design and construction of the first really practical tandem. This machine was constructed on the cross-frame principle with a single diagonal backbone which, because of its low rear-riding position, made it suitable for a woman rider. The first model had coupled steering for both handlebars, but that was abandoned after tests showed that the arrangement was wrong in principle. The machine was successful as far as practicality and construction were concerned, but it was never made in large enough quantities to prove itself.

Compared with Rucker's American design, Albone's foresaw the advent of the long wheelbase form of tandem, from which the double-diamond frame eventually evolved to become the accepted standard in tandems.

In 1889, A. G. Spalding and Brothers imported a combination tandem called the Ivel from England to America and sold it for two hundred dollars. It was regarded as the ideal tandem for a lady and gentleman. In 1897, the Raleigh tandem was another fine example of this early form. Again it was publicized as being suitable for both sexes to ride. Arnold, Schwinn and Company was among the first American manufacturing firms to see the possibility of the tandem as a romantic vehicle. Another of their models, popular in 1897, was a long wheelbase tandem with a seat specially built in for a small child.

The early designers never seem to have the same expertise in designing tandems that they showed in designing bicycles for one person. It was not merely a matter of lengthening a cycle and providing it with two seats; entirely new designs had to be achieved, with points of stress taken into consideration. Time plus ingenuity provided the answer. After Rucker's machine, Dan Albone's, and Raleigh Company designs, the flaws were slowly eliminated. However, the tandem was never as popular as the bicycle.

Once the bugs were out, it was easier to design multiple machines for three, four, five, six, seven, even ten seats. One of the earliest known examples of extraordinarily large bicycles was built by the Waltham Manufacturing Company of Massachusetts in 1896. They produced the Decemtuple, which created a sensation when it was sent on tour to Europe. Under favorable conditions, it could achieve one mile a minute. The Decemtuple is now the property of the Henry Ford Museum and may be seen at Dearborn, Michigan. On one occasion, ten intrepid ladies rode the Decemtuple in a trial run of fifty

The world's largest bicycle, built in 1968, is 35¼ feet long, weighs more than half a ton, and seats twenty-one riders.

Courtesy Hares Garage, Hampshire, England

miles' duration. It must have been quite a sight in those days when women were supposed to be "the weaker sex"!

From time to time, there has been a craze in Europe to produce bicycles to carry more and more people. Such machines are popular attractions for carnivals and the English-style country fairs. The Rickman brothers of Hampshire, England, built a mammoth twenty-one-seat bicycle that was 35¼ feet long and weighed over half a ton! On August 5, 1968, it established a world record as the longest bicycle in the world, but since that date, a few modifications have been made on it. The power is now supplied by twelve men instead of eight. The cranks have been replaced by twenty-four sprockets and a hundred feet of chain. The drive goes through a motorcycle gearbox and clutch to a single chain at the rear wheel.

The brakes, too, have been improved, which must be consoling to its riders. The driver has a foot brake hydraulically operated on the rear disk. There are also lights and indicators at the front and rear, and in case this rare multicycle is not noticed, it also has an earsplitting horn. The mammoth cycle is now owned by Nicholas Hare of Littlehampton, England. Apart from being a popular attraction at carnivals, the machine also makes goodwill tours abroad as an ambassador of craftsmanship. Enthusiastic members of the Rickman Engineering Company gave their leisure hours to combine their skills and make this machine. It must have given every member of the team a lot of personal satisfaction when they tested it on the Thruxton Road Race Circuit Track and completed a lap of the four-mile circuit, under their own pedal power, in twenty-five minutes.

In Hampshire, on June 23, 1972, the world's heaviest bicycle had a successful run, pedaled by twenty girls. This is a thirty-five-foot-long giant weighing two tons! It actually seats twenty-two people, but two of the school girls dropped out when the run was made, which was not surprising. The sight of such an enormous pedal vehicle must inevitably give rise to a few misgivings about its safety. This machine has been used to raise money for charities, and in 1972 was often seen in the resort area of Teignmouth in Devonshire, England, which is famous for its small, winding roads. The chairman of the Teignmouth Council reported that the giant cycle ran well enough, but he admitted that the riders had trouble when meeting a bus. It is also hard work to pedal the machine—or even to get it moving! But once everyone is synchronized, it certainly can move. The monster cycle cost $2,500 to build, which seems to be a reasonable price considering the amount of metal in it.

The bicycle has always appealed to the special type of humor that many inventors possess. A barber in Coney Island in 1920 provided himself with a traveling barbershop by mounting a barber's chair on a tricycle, and rode around the countryside plying his trade. A report about his strange but practical device states that he had a small box attached containing a variety of shaving mugs and pomades—"wherefrom the rustic population may receive the proper hirsute attendance from this novel and wholly unprecedented artist."

In Berlin, Germany, the owner of a tobacco shop made a large display counter out of a box and placed it on wheels. In 1899 it must have been a great attraction to the populace to see the tobacco merchant pedaling his goods to his clients in the streets of Berlin. He liked night riding and devised an electric sign for the top of the box, with a storage battery tucked away below.

The immigration of Italians to the United States just before the turn of the century brought the street piano, known as the hurdy-gurdy, into popularity. A New York manufacturer of street pianos decided that he could expand his trade by mounting a piano on a tricycle. After that, itinerant musicians,

These French posters were quick to capture the romance of the new sport of cycling.

Courtesy Montagu Motor Museum, Beaulieu, Hants., England

often complete with pet monkeys to attract the crowd, could travel into the countryside. A commentator of the time wrote, "As the idea is a novelty and as the transportation from place to place will virtually cost him nothing except an extra expenditure of muscle, this genius (the inventor) ought soon to lay up a competence." There is no record that the New York manufacturer became a millionaire, but the hurdy-gurdy certainly brought a lot of pleasure to people outside the towns.

Street vending was once the easiest way for an immigrant to earn a living. Since he rarely came from Europe to the United States with any kind of fortune, he could not afford a regular shop—but he knew a lot about the art of salesmanship. Survival instincts were high in immigrants. They added color to the areas in which they settled and brought many new ideas. Selling foodstuffs was the most popular type of vending, and each nationality had its own specialty. There were Italian ice-cream vendors and the Jewish bagel sellers. One man had a flair for dispensing pink lemonade and snowballs. He mounted a water cooler on a child's tricycle and pushed his vehicle around. Then he decided he might just as well ride as walk, and at the same time expand his business. So he mounted a soda fountain on a chain-driven bicycle and became the first mechanized soda jerk!

The phonograph was invented in 1877 by Thomas Edison, and in 1885, C. A. Bell and C. S. Tainter patented the first improvements on the machine and called it the Gramophone. Two years later Émile Berliner developed a different method of sound recording, which used a flat disk, a vast improvement over the earlier cylinder type. Berliner's machine was also called a Gramophone. It was easy enough to mount either of these on a bicycle and so to take music to the public and earn a few dollars by passing the hat around.

The last decade of the nineteenth century is full of stories of whimsical uses being made of bicycles and tricycles. Several types of bicycle boats were built and operated successfully, although their popularity was short-lived. The public loves any novelty or variation on a popular theme, but they are also very fickle. One of the earliest bicycle boats was Hales Water Velocipede, invented by an Englishman. As illustrated in a catalog of 1889, it was a neat affair very much like a miniature steamboat.

Another bicycle boat was shown in the December 21, 1895, issue of the *Scientific American*. The article stated that un-skilled riders could propel the boat a five miles an hour, and that ladies could relax while safely leaving the hard work to a man. In the same year, an early catamaran-type bicycle boat was invented by Don Ramón Barea of Madrid, Spain. The machine was composed of two cases of steel, which served as floats and were connected by crossbars. In the space between the two and near the stern, there was a paddlelike wheel operated by pedals. The nautical bicycle weighed one hundred pounds and Don Barea demonstrated its capabilities himself. He passed over the water on the machine at a speed of six miles an hour. The strange contraption was steered by a small rudder at the stern. A magazine called *La Ilustracion Española y Americana* suggested that it would be specially suited to lakes and rivers, adding: "It is well spoken of in Paris." In those days, any invention that was approved by the French Academy of Sciences was considered to have the official seal of approval.

Bicycle boats became very popular in Boston, especially one variety known as "swan boats" because of their shape. They are still in operation there in the Public Garden. They have a catamaran hull and a bicycle mechanism minus wheels. The chain drive is attached to a rear paddle. Several passengers can be accommodated on seats. Swan boats have become quite an American institution, comparable to the carrousel.

From whimsies providing either a means of making a living

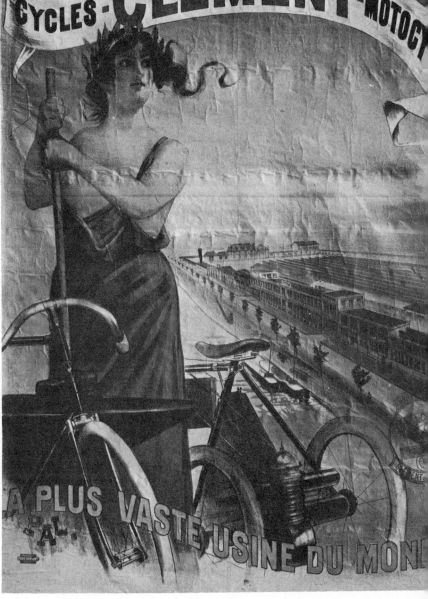

"Women on wheels." The bicycle helped pave the way toward women's liberation.

Courtesy Montagu Motor Museum, Beaulieu, Hants., England

or giving pleasure to people during their leisure hours, it is not a far cry to producing freaks. The purpose of freak bicycles cannot be clearly defined except that they probably fulfill some hidden sense of derring-do in the inventors and a desire to be an exhibitionist. One such freak was called the Eiffel Tower bicycle. There were two versions of this machine; one was built on a single bicycle frame, the other on a tandem. From the single bicycle rose a ten-foot-high frame on which a man could sit while being driven by his partner below. The tandem had a twenty-foot-high frame and was driven by two men, with one or more other men clinging perilously to the top of the twenty-foot frame. Both versions were practically impossible to ride, but there is always someone who is ready to try anything that has an element of danger in it. The Eiffel Tower bicycle never appeared in a circus act but was simply a freak of its time.

There was no Society for the Prevention of Cruelty to Animals in 1895 in Strasbourg, when a gentleman devised a strange addition to his tricycle. In order not to use his own energy, he invented an attachment at the rear of the machine. Into this, one or two dogs could be fitted to provide propulsion for the vehicle and its rider. The man who invented a carrier for his bicycle so that his pet could accompany him on rides was more humane. Such a means of transport for pet and master is often seen today, but it is not wise to try it on busy roads. Pets have to be very well trained to ride in a carrier on a bicycle, and many states have laws forbidding the carrying of an extra passenger on a bicycle, whether it is a four-footed friend or a small brother.

One of the strangest of these whimsical inventions was that designed by James Edward Leahan of Boston, Massachusetts. He called it the Leahan's Ice Velocipede. Apparently Mr. Leahan enjoyed the times when the Charles River was frozen. He then removed the wheels of his bicycle and replaced the back one with a spiked wheel. There were two semicircular side flanges that rubbed along the ice and another one that replaced the front wheel. The rider/skater presumably got up speed by means of the spiked wheel and then just coasted along.

The bicycle roller skate was a phenomenon of 1901. Two small wheels were linked by springs, and the skater strapped his foot on the top of the springboard. Stopping was provided for by a crude sort of braking rod. This chain-driven invention was the brainchild of Paul Jassman of Brooklyn. Strangely enough, a miniature bicycle attached to skating boots became quite popular around that time, and appeared in several catalogs, including one issued by A. G. Spalding and Brothers.

The bicycle even invaded the railroad field when a Mr. Thompson designed a speed booster that he used in a vehicle known as the Thompson Propelling Mechanism. The principle was that he applied a flywheel to a velocipede on rails. It was operated on both road and rail in 1896 and for a few years afterward. Then it fell into disuse—killed by a lack of interest.

Also in 1896 the Leamy Revolving Trapeze act played at the Olympia Music Hall in New York and delighted large audiences. It was the vaudeville hit of the season. A woman on a bicycle generated enough energy to send her two companions flying around on huge trapezes. In addition, switches near the handlebars turned on colored electric lights that provided the equivalent of a strobe effect on the scene high above the circus floor. Trick cyclists are still a major feature in many circuses.

Although it is basically a simple machine, the bicycle is versatile. It can function on water and ice and in the air. It can stretch itself to extremes and accommodate more than two dozen riders, or it can be miniaturized and still work. It can be ridden by people of any age and of any size and weight. P. T. Barnum, the great circus impresario, had a velocipede built for his famous midget, Charles Sherwood Stratton (better known as General Tom Thumb). This tiny and historically interesting cycle can be seen in the Henry Ford Museum.

Everyone who has ever owned a bicycle has known the thrill of freedom it can give. The "curious invention" of Baron von Drais came, was seen, and was tried out. Ultimately it conquered the hearts of people all over the world.

CHAPTER SIX

SYMBOL OF A REBELLIOUS AGE

Although today the cyclist must battle with cars for his place on the roads of the world, it was actually the bicycle that helped to launch the age of the automobile. Americans of the 1890's took to the craze of bicycling, and that led to the construction of better roads. The early cyclists had to face heavily rutted roads, which were much more hazardous for them than for horses and carriages. So they organized clubs and pressured civic officials to build better roads. Without these roads, the bicycle could never have survived to make such an impact on society. Hiram P. Maxim, a prominent American inventor, wrote:

> It was the bicycle that first directed men's minds to the possibilities of independent long-distance travel over the ordinary highway. . . . We could have built automobiles in 1880 or even 1870, but we delayed because the bicycle had not yet come in numbers and had not turned our minds to the idea of a "horseless carriage."

During the peak of the bicycle boom in 1895, Americans spent over a hundred million dollars on their vehicles! In France, the number of cyclists soared from a mere five thousand in 1890 to over ten million by 1900. It was the same all over Europe. With millions of cyclists clamoring for the right to have good roads to ride on and with powerful clubs like the League of American Wheelmen adding their voices to the clamor, it was inevitable that better roads had to be built. On June 15, 1895, twin cycle paths were opened in Brooklyn from Prospect Park to Coney Island, and on weekends, it is said, there was tire-to-tire traffic as cyclists made their way to the famed amusement area.

The Pasadena and Los Angeles Cycleway was one of the great freeways in the world. Charles F. Holder wrote about the cycleway in the July 14, 1900, issue of the *Scientific American:*

> The Pasadena and Los Angeles cycleway is a movement to provide the wheelman with a perfect road, with a minimum grade between two cities nine miles apart and at different altitudes. . . . The cycleway, which it is believed is the only one of its kind in the world, is an elevated, perfectly adjusted road running from the heart of Pasadena to the plaza of Los Angeles. In appearance it somewhat resembles the elevated road in New York, being apparently as high in places; but it is built of wood instead of iron, yet strong enough to bear the equipment and car service of an electric road . . . in brief, when the cycleway is complete, it will be twice as wide, which warrants the assumption that the promoters may have some additional object in view— something else than to afford wheelmen and wheelwomen a perfect road. Whether this is true has not been given out, but a few days ago an automobile owned by a resident of Pasadena, was run out upon the cycleway and went speeding toward Los Angeles under the most perfect conditions; and it was evident that if the road permitted an automobile to run upon it, it would soon become very popular as a literal sky route to Los Angeles for these vehicles.

Boston, called the Athens of America, had an abundance of parks and cycleways, while Michigan Avenue in Chicago literally bustled with activity as the sporting types of the town developed a taste for the new sport. The Americans of the Gay Nineties had a vision of the future as they foresaw the need for better roads.

Americans went through a brief period of being on speaking terms with the velocipede, but it was the Centennial Exposition in Philadelphia in 1876 that helped to launch the bicycle in the United States. Several English manufacturers exhibited their Ordinary cycles at this exhibition. Colonel Albert A. Pope, an officer in the Civil War, went to Europe and, with great sense and determination, purchased the patent rights to produce Ordinary cycles in the United States. He made the first one in 1877 in Boston, but in 1878 contracted with the Weed Sewing Machine Company of Hartford, Connecticut, to manufacture bicycles. At the same time the trade name of Columbia came into use.

The manufacture of the Ordinary bicycle was short-lived, though, because news filtered across the Atlantic that the new safety bicycles were going to be better than the Ordinary cycles. The Smith Machine Company of Smithtown, New Jersey, patented the design for a safety bicycle on November 23, 1880, and then exhibited it at a meeting of the League of American Wheelmen in Boston on May 30, 1881. The machine was called, appropriately enough, the American Star. The Eagle Manufacturing Company put out a pamphlet giving instruction on how to mount these complicated mechanical giraffes, and was also careful to give details about "Dismounting" and "Learning how to Fall." Indeed, after reading the pamphlet, a potential purchaser of a high-wheel bicycle is likely to have had second thoughts.

About 1890 the Knight Cycle Company of St. Louis, Missouri, brought out the Bronco, describing it as a light roadster. It was so closely coupled, with the saddle almost on top of the handlebars, that one can only hope that this company also gave some riding instructions to its buyers. The design looks pleasing enough on paper, but when a human body was added to this bicycle, it was apt to tip over backward. It was in the price range of $135 to $150. The Bronco was a modified Ordinary bicycle, and although there are no records of how many riders were thrown because of the short coupling, at least it alerted the United States to the need of changing to the safety bicycle, which was now gaining ground in Europe.

In 1892 the Overman Wheel Company became one of the earliest American makers of safety bicycles. They produced a line of bicycles called Victor, as well as a unique, if slightly bizarre, creation called the Racquette, which had a frame resembling a tennis racket. In the same year, John F. Palmer of Chicago came along with the answer to strengthening the Dunlop pneumatic tire. He perfected a cotton-cord tire, which is basically the same type of tire we use today, not only on bicycles but also on automobiles and aircraft, except that man-made materials like nylon and rayon are now employed in it instead of cotton.

The first National Bicycle Show was held in New York City's Madison Square Garden in 1895 and attracted a great deal of attention. The star of the show was a Tribune weighing only 8¾ pounds. It had 28-inch wheels and a 43¾-inch wheelbase. In Europe, most manufacturers were still concerned with

The "new woman" in America took great interest in the bicycle craze in the Gay Nineties.

Courtesy Montague Motor Museum, Beaulieu, Hants., England

HURTU

DILIGEON & C.ie

Imp. LEMERCIER, 57, rue de Seine, Paris

54. Rue St. Maur · **PARIS** · 33. Bd Sébastopol

The bicycle provided a new means of freedom for daring young ladies at the turn of the twentieth century.

producing bicycles that combined speed with safety, and they always had difficulty in reducing the weight of the best bicycles. Therefore, it is surprising that, despite all the "Ohs" and "Ahs" of the public visiting the national show, the Tribune never attained commercial success.

When comparing the story of the bicycle in Europe with its American counterpart, one can have no doubt that European manufacturers (particularly those in England) had the edge on evolving designs. But the United States added its own special and unique quality of showmanship, which helped enormously in popularizing the vehicle. The American manufacturers were also good at improving the basic English bicycles. In some cases they seemed to overdo it, and perhaps that was what defeated the Tribune in the commercial sense. The featherweight was too extreme and people felt it would not stand the strain of regular riding by a person weighing, say, one hundred and fifty pounds.

The Gay Nineties were also the Naughty Nineties, and the bicycle fitted beautifully into a decade that was revolting in every way against ancestral puritanism, because the bicycle brought with it a sense of freedom. It was too soon for the hysteria over the automobile and for ten or more glorious years, the bicycle flourished.

In 1895 the Eastern Rubber Company used a dashing young lady mounted on a bicycle as part of their advertising campaign. Daringly she showed her skirts tucked well up to the knees. Magazines showed fashion models on bicycles and the great comic-opera diva Lillian Russell made news when she cycled through New York's Washington Park. Racycle Bicycle Company used her picture in one of their publicity campaigns.

A common practice in Butte, Montana, was for a trolley car belonging to the railway company to take parties of cyclists into what is now ski country. Provision was made for the bicycles to hang outside the trolley car while their owners had the comfort of riding up the mountainside, presumably so they could cycle downhill. It worked rather like the present-day ski lift.

The Gay Nineties was the decade of families going out to picnic at such places as Bedford Rest in Brooklyn or Grant's Tomb on Riverside Drive in Manhattan. The most noticeable thing about the advent of bicycles in America was the interest women took in the craze. Many more years passed in Europe before women were accepted as cyclists, but their American counterparts took to the bicycle like ducks to water. Those who could not afford to buy special clothes tucked up their skirts and pedaled gallantly into the twentieth century.

With woman at the helm—or rather at the handlebars—the next step was to develop a whole new look in fashion geared to the sport. The designers of the Gay Nineties seem to have managed to merge practicality with panache in much the same way designers of ski clothes do today. Blouses with leg-of-mutton sleeves, bloomers (baggy pantaloons worn with a knee-length skirt, invented by Amelia Bloomer in the 1850's), divided skirts, and exotic versions of long johns were worn by lady cyclists. Men sported knickers, knee-length hose, and Tyrolean hats. All these daring new clothes brought a special kind of American craziness to the cult of the bicycle.

But puritanism was not dead; it stalked the cyclists as they thronged to Coney Island and the Pasadena cycleway. The main grievance was that the bicycles were out in full force on the weekends, including Sundays. Picnics were all-day affairs because the cyclists started early in the morning and made their way leisurely toward their various favorite places. There, fun and frolic were the order of the day—with bicycles parked against trees while the riders gathered in groups, perhaps listening to someone playing a concertina, while others spread out their sandwiches and drank Coca-Cola or beer.

Clergymen thundered from their pulpits against the latest craze, which was keeping people from attending their churches; cyclists were pedaling their way to perdition, hell-fire, and ultimate damnation, they claimed. Of course all sports were frowned on when they were organized on Sundays, but previously people had seemed more able to compromise by going to church in the morning first. The bicycle took people away from their homes right out into the country, and so the clergy berated it more enthusiastically than other sports.

Some people, of course, actually used their bicycles to take them to church, but this did not make them immune to the scoldings of outraged gentlemen of the cloth. Women riding astride a bicycle, sometimes in unfeminine clothes, added fuel to the fiery rage.

The churches in Europe were more tolerant of the bicycle than those in the United States, probably because Americans used their bicycles mainly as a form of leisure, while Europeans used theirs as a means of getting to work.

The puritans were never noted for their sense of humor or their ability to appreciate a zest for living. In America the innocent bicycle touched a sensitive area of religious thought and, to some extent, broke the control of many a clergyman. The amazing thing is that the heavens did not fall, any more than they do today when young people grow long hair, strum on guitars, and create rock operas based on the life of Jesus Christ.

The Gay Nineties came and went, but they left an indelible mark, and succeeding generations remember the period with nostalgia.

CHAPTER SEVEN

THE BICYCLE RIDES INTO THE TWENTIETH CENTURY

Over a period of 150 years, the bicycle has evolved from being a rich man's whimsical toy to a machine of tremendous precision and beauty. The bicycle is one of man's most important inventions. Its basic design and shape have changed little since 1900. In that year the bicycle was the only inexpensive and convenient type of personal transport available. It had been adopted by increasing numbers of people of all classes and had become an essential part of human life for commercial and utilitarian purposes. The safety bicycle had become so refined that some of the best examples of workmanship came out during this period. There was also a great deal of choice for buyers, although three broad classes were constantly produced.

1. Special cycles built by local manufacturers in comparatively small quantities.
2. More and more mass-produced bicycles made by the large manufacturers, all of which combined sound design with economy in production, and so could be sold for realistic prices, bringing them within the range of the buying power of the workingman.

CONSTRUITS
par les Ateliers
DE PETIT BOURG
PRÈS
PARIS
CYCLES

BICYCLETTES DE LUXE
BICYCLETTES POPULAIRE
LES PLUS PERFECTIONNÉES
LES MIEUX CONSTRUITES
Envoi Franco
du Catalogue illustré

DECAUVILLE

FABRICATION FRANÇAISE

Adresser les Commandes 13, Bould MALESHERBES, PARIS

(Téléphone) Adresse Télégraphique: DECAUVILLE PARIS

3. Deluxe machines, superbly made, especially for discerning—and often eccentric—clients without any regard to cost.

The first deluxe bicycle was also one of the most unorthodox; it was called the Dursley-Pederson. Although the frame design was patented in 1893, this special bicycle was not made until about 1902. The frame was completely triangulated, which was unusual, because the diamond frame was in vogue. It was assembled in such a way that every tubular member was subjected to compression strain only. The saddle was made from light matting and was similar in appearance to a miniature hammock. The whole bicycle weighed only fourteen pounds, which was enough to make it unique. It was the sensation of its day and became very popular. It was so well made that there are records of people buying one and using it for fifty years with little or no cost for maintenance repairs.

Marston Sunbeam, Lea-Francis, and Beeston Humber were companies that produced excellent deluxe models embodying the highest qualities of design, materials, manufacture, and finish—combined with superior efficiency and durability. The great majority of the now standard safety bicycles offered for sale between 1900 and 1910 were the products of old, established companies such as Baylis and Thomas, New Hudson, Humber, BSA, Rudge-Whitworth, Raleigh, Triumph, Swift, and Alldays and Onions. They all offered machines of good quality within a price range of from fifteen to fifty dollars.

The average weight of a touring bicycle was from thirty-five to forty pounds, while sports models were about thirty pounds. A variety of saddles sprang up, ranging from the hard

Our ancestors were quicker to understand the advantages of the pedal-powered wheeled vehicle than we are today.

The Dursley-Pederson, one of the first lightweight deluxe bicycles, 1905.

Courtesy Art Gallery and Museum, Glasgow, Scotland

ones for racing to the well-sprung broad types for touring. For an additional price, a vast range of accessories could be added to the standard models.

By the time the Dursley Pederson deluxe model appeared, it seemed there was nothing left for a bicycle designer to achieve, and very few innovations can be found between 1902 and 1925. The First World War (1914–1918) was partially responsible for this stagnation because companies like the Birmingham Small Arms had to put their skills, manpower, and production efforts into making armaments.

But now a major menace was slowly making itself felt. Automobiles and motorcycles were being used more and more and seemed likely to deal the deathblow to bicycles just as they had reached the peak of perfection. The same type of inventive mind that year after year had met the challenge of creating better bicycles was now turning to cars. The internal-combustion machine offered greater speed and, in addition, could transport a whole family in comfort. At first, as with the early bicycles, cost was the major factor holding back the avalanche of would-be car buyers who, in time, would defect from the joys of bicycling. As usual, the wealthy were the first to take up the new fad, but then Henry Ford came along with his Model T and placed the automobile within the price range of most Americans.

Moderate quantities of safety bicycles were still being produced each year, but always as standardized models. After 1925, there came a new flurry of excitement as mass production methods were applied to bicycles. At the same time new materials came on the market and the old companies manufacturing bicycles saw the advantages of using them.

The production of various steels of substantially improved strength—in conjunction with better techniques in brazing, silver soldering, and welding—made it possible to reduce the weight of bicycles still further while keeping the frames adequately stiff and strong. A shorter wheelbase was evolved, and a more upright steering head resulted in a compact type of machine. Wheels of 26 inches in diameter, with tires measuring from 1¼ inches to 1⅜ inches, became standard, together with lighter fittings and accessories.

Celluloid was used for such items as mudguards, chain cases, and chain guards. In handlebars and pedals, which took only moderate stress, light alloys took the place of the heavier metals such as steel. True, a chrome molybdenum or manganese-molybdenum alloy of steel had been tried in 1920, but

Whitworth Cycles

IMPRIMERIE. PAUL DUPONT, 4, R. du Bouloi, Paris

These posters advertise the advantages of the new lightweight bicycles in a most persuasive way.

Courtesy Montagu Motor Museum, Beaulieu, Hants., England

while it increased strength, it did not reduce the weight. It took another war to bring new improvements in alloys which, in time, would increase strength while allowing for reduced weight.

The history of the evolution of the bicycle is full of man's awareness of what is needed, but often the inventive mind is ahead of the necessary technology required to produce the final article.

In the first half of the twentieth century many people shook their heads and gloomily foresaw the complete demise of the bicycle because of the growing love for the automobile. Certainly it did look that way in the United States, where the bicycle became only a child's toy, to be cast aside for a car at the proper age. In Europe, however, wise manufacturers knew there would always be a market for bicycles as long as men went out to work. The class system in Europe is much more substantial than in the United States and, to this day, the standard of living is not based on need for every family to have a car in order to survive. The European workingman and his family proved to be the mainstay of the bicycle industry, even when he could afford a car as well.

Born of necessity, the mother of invention, the bicycle was here to stay—but it had to learn to live with the automobile.

CHAPTER EIGHT

THE BICYCLE IN
TIME OF WAR

In a special bicycle issue of *Harper's Magazine* of April 11, 1896, there appeared this paragraph:

> It is in rapidly moving considerable bodies of infantry that the bicycle will find its highest function in time of war. Fancy a force of infantry, independent of roads and railroads, moving in any direction, forty or fifty miles in one morning, and appearing on a field not weary and exhausted after a two days' march, but fresh and prepared to fight. . . .

This was practically the first formal indication of the role the bicycle could play in military maneuvers. Military men of the time envisioned the bicycle as an invaluable machine for outpost duties and for scouting, and a few officers were trained to use bicycles as part of their inspection duties.

However, the United States was not the first country to have this idea. In 1870 the Italian Army furnished each regiment of its infantry, grenadiers, sappers and miners, engineers, and cavalry with four bicycles apiece. One can only imagine what the diehard cavalry officers thought of the bicycle! Each machine was equipped with brakes, lantern, rifle support, leather pouch for orders, and a knapsack.

In 1885 bicycle-mounted Austrian soldiers bearing a full field kit were doing a hundred miles a day on field maneuvers, far exceeding anything the cavalry could do on horseback.

The major disadvantage of the military use of bicycles was that the solid, or cushion, tires did not function well over rough land. But the pneumatic tire developed by Dunlop in 1888 made a vast difference.

France, always prepared to make its own innovative contributions, produced a crude form of "folding bicycle" in 1896. It weighed only twenty-three pounds and could be carried on a soldier's back.

The first branch of the American military to use the bicycle was the National Guard of Connecticut, but eventually the Army Signal Corps and other divisions of the military began to take up its use too. Some were deployed in twos to take small cannons; others were equipped with rifles and field packs; one was used with a machine gun; yet another had a Colt rapid-firing machine gun mounted on its handlebars.

In the last decade of the nineteenth century, many civilians were riding bicycles, and soldiers were also instructed how to ride. This practice accelerated until the present day. The United States Military Wheelmen, a volunteer auxiliary force of the National Guard, trained soldiers on bicycles. In 1896 a Lieutenant Whitney issued this statement:

> The balance of power is so nicely adjusted that the chances in the coming conflict will be governed by efficiency in detailed preparation. The bicycle will weigh in the scale. We are told somewhere that for want of a horseshoe nail a battle was lost. In the next war, for want of a bicycle the independence of a nation may be forfeited.

The good lieutenant was something of a prophet.

Also in 1896 Captain R. E. Thompson of the United States Signal Corps saw the possibility of using a bicycle to pay out and retrieve telegraph and telephone wire. With the attachment he invented, a bicycle could run out a third of a mile of wire and retrieve it within two minutes. A German inventor named Leo Kamm worked out a similar device. Kamm also attached a bell to his invention that would warn the bicycle operator to stop before the wire was fully played out.

In 1897 at the Northwestern Military Academy of Lake Geneva, Wisconsin, an officer in charge, Royal Page Davidson, organized a corps of sixteen cadets complete with sixteen standard bicycles. Each bicycle was capable of carrying rifles and other military gear. One of the tests for the bicycle cadets was to scale a wall carrying their machines—plus forty-five pounds of equipment! Under Davidson, other maneuvers were carried out, including cross-country runs. On June 7, 1897, these sixteen cadets left Chicago to deliver a message to the Secretary of State in Washington, D.C. The journey, via the National Pike road, took nineteen days.

Stimulated by the interest of Davidson, the United States Army asked the Pope Manufacturing Company to develop a bicycle on which a Colt automatic machine gun could be carried. The Pope Company improved on this by manufacturing a tandem mounted with a twelve-shot repeating rifle, two Colt quick-action revolvers, a case of signal flags, two rolled overcoats, and two blankets. The tandem was actually the usual civilian model, and the secret lay in the effective placement of the military paraphernalia.

The Boer War broke out in Africa in 1899, and now the bicycle really came into its own as a viable war vehicle. The English company of Dursley Pederson, once known as makers of the ultimate in deluxe bicycles, designed one that could be folded up; it weighed only fifteen pounds. A soldier could easily carry the machine on his back when the roads were too rough for riding.

When World War I broke out in 1914, the bicycle proved to be a valuable asset as a mount for the infantry. The folding variety was used by French troops as they made their way from village to village. Horses, of course, were then used a great deal in war, but they had to be fed. Also, they were regarded as the special property of the cavalry. The infantry corps could move just as quickly by using the bicycle.

A German doctor invented the velocipede ambulance, and in some instances it displaced the horse, usually used for that task. He put his vehicle to use at the Royal Charity Hospital in Berlin, where it was found to be a speedy and comfortable means of getting patients to the hospital. It was also very economical.

In World War I, the Allies had a special cycle corps, which did valiant work on the battlefield and also in maintaining liaison with outposts.

During the Second World War the bicycle saved many lives, simply because it was the most common means of transport and attracted less attention than a car. Refugees escaping from Germany used bicycles whenever possible. Because it was an easier way to slip across frontiers, the bicycle became the most popular getaway machine. In any case, there was a gasoline shortage during the Second World War, so the automobile, once the king of the road, became practically obsolete, giving the bicycle its chance to make a big comeback.

The famous underground movement of France, called the Maquis, was a group of citizens who quietly went about their work in the daytime as civilians and then organized escapes for fleeing prisoners at night. Many escaped from Occupied France by using bicycles. A special kind of anonymity comes to bicycle riders in time of war—they look innocent. When a hunted man rides a bicycle in a crowd of people who are all doing the same thing, he is not likely to be noticed.

When paratroopers were dropped in occupied territory, many of them were equipped with a fine version of the folding bicycle, which could be assembled easily and so enabled the men to disappear silently and quickly into the countryside. Because of the mobility of the bicycle, they could make use of small footpaths and keep away from the main highways, which usually were infested with enemy troop movements.

When a pseudopeace came to the world at the end of World War II, old and faithful bicycles were not packed away in barns or garages. The European public had discovered the true usefulness of the bicycle, and it was to remain for them a means of economical personal transport. However, in the United States, which did not have all the horrors of war on its immediate doorstep, it was easier for people to take up a way of life in which the automobile played an increasingly important part.

CHAPTER NINE

THE BICYCLE
IN PEACETIME

Bicycles with high wheels had been used mainly by men, and as late as 1885, some people considered it unladylike to ride a bicycle. A young lady wrote to a magazine in that year and got the following answer to her question about the propriety of women riding a bicycle: "The mere act of riding a bicycle is not in itself sinful and if it is the only means of reaching the church on Sunday it may be excusable. . . ."

When the tricycle made its appearance, people considered it more respectable than the bicycle, and it appealed to women because of its greater stability. The Cyclists Touring Club (founded as the Bicycle Touring Club in 1878), entered into serious discussion about what kinds of dress a woman could wear while bicycling and still remain a lady. They suggested a woolen garment next to the skin, a pair of dark-gray woolen stockings, and a pair of loose knickerbockers fastened with elastic under the knee.

Women began to defy the tradition of always wearing skirts, and some wildly designed clothes suitable for women bicyclists began to appear. One, called the "rational dress" in Europe, consisted of knickerbockers, long leggings, and a coat long enough to look feminine without interfering with movement.

111

The Lady Cyclists Association was formed in 1892 and strongly recommended the adoption of "rational dress," but there was an instance where a hotel in Europe refused to serve women bicyclists. It became a *cause célèbre* when their cases went to court. The hotel owner was acquitted, but the event became one of many milestones on the road to female emancipation.

However, bicycles provided the only means of getting away from home without the effort of walking, so more and more women were determined to use them. Bicycles acquired a mark of respectability when clergymen's wives and daughters began to use them, and gradually the machine brought about a change in manners. The use of the bicycle by women signaled the end of the age-old tradition of chaperones, those middle-aged ladies who always escorted young women wherever they went. A young lady could escape to keep her secret tryst with a lover and still be home for afternoon tea while innocently protesting that she had just been for a bicycle ride to take cookies to a relation or to collect wild flowers to press.

Indeed, an anonymous poet wrote in "The Passoniate Cyclist and His Love":

> Come ride with me and be my love
> And I will all the pleasures prove
> Of sauntering in the shady lanes
> Where golden-tinted summer reigns. . . .

Many a young Victorian lady used her bicycle as a means to a romantic adventure.

Magazine writers viewed bicycling women with gloom and foreboding, and a famous British author, Mrs. Harcourt Williamson, became really alarmed and waxed imaginative at the new trend for bicycling:

Parents and guardians will probably only be wise after the event. Given a lonely road and a tramp desperate with hunger or naturally vicious, and it stands to reason that a girl, or indeed a woman, riding alone must be in some considerable peril.

There are grownups with this point of view in every generation. Our grandmothers suffered just as much in their teen-age years as many young people do today. To be young is to invite suspicion!

The bicycle paved the way toward the freedom which today's young people accept as a right. They forget that our grandmothers paid a price and threw in their dime's worth to buy freedom at a time when all a young woman could hope for was to get married to a suitor approved by her parents.

With the advent of bicycling clubs, another bastion fell to women. In the past clubs had belonged exclusively to men, but the bicycle sped through the doors of the clubs and they became open to members of both sexes.

The clubs were instrumental in getting new legislation passed concerning bicycles, and the Cyclists Touring Club of Great Britain played a large part in this. Bicyclists wanted to establish the status of their machines as carriages, so that they could use the highways without fear of being prosecuted. After a vigorous and skillfully waged campaign, the club achieved a notable victory by means of an amendment of the Local Government Bill introduced in the British Houses of Parliament in 1888. The bill became law the same year because people from all over the country bombarded their government members. It was a great legal milestone in cycling history and earned the name "Magna Charta for Cyclists."

The Act stated that "bicycles, tricycles, velocipedes and other similar machines are hereby declared to be carriages within the meaning of the Act." It gave bicyclists the right to

use the roads without hindrance from local authorities, and also paved the way for the club to keep a watchful eye on future legislation. Many local authorities tried to deny bicyclists the right, even up to 1950, but the club's amendment was strong, and has to date been virtually unbreakable.

When women took to the road in force, many were brought into the courts to be accused of "improper dress and conduct," and again the bicycling clubs came out in strong defense of women's rights. Gradually, clubs sprang up all over Europe, each a child of the British Cyclists Touring Club, which has always been recognized as the leader in all matters pertaining to the bicycle.

The club also initiated a system of accident insurance for bicyclists and played a part in the development of a bicycling proficiency scheme, inaugurated by the Royal Society for the Prevention of Accidents, with the full support of the ministries of Education and Transport. This is an area which the United States clubs must ultimately get into as the number of bicyclists increases in this country. Unfortunately, the United States still regards the bicycle as little more than a child's toy, although actual sales prove that this is not so. More and more adults are taking up bicycling, and they must soon realize that they have rights on the road too, and that they should not be relegated to the place of second-class citizens while the all-powerful car owners dominate the scene.

In this country, we are still far behind in the use of the bicycle, chiefly because the United States has been a much more affluent country than any of the European ones. In Europe, the friendly figure of the local mailman making his

The Paramount, one of the finest ten-speed tandems made by the famous American company of Arnold, Schwinn & Co.

rounds on his officially issued bicycle is a common enough scene. The police in England use bicycles, again officially issued by the government. Many men and women go to work on bicycles, and many children use them to get to school. There are very few families, even among the wealthy, who have two cars—but they always have bicycles. The district nurses, a fine feature of rural European life, use bicycles, and seem able to cope with distressing weather conditions without turning a hair. The district nurses are also midwives, and many a pregnant woman has heaved a sigh of relief at the sight of her nurse arriving on her bicycle.

All over the world, whenever the need for personal transport has cropped up, the bicycle was the first thing to be introduced. Laborers in Africa use bicycles, and they use a great deal of imaginative ingenuity to keep their vehicles on the road. The prime motive for using bicycles in every country, except the United States, is always economics, because the bicycle is the only inexpensive way to transport people from home to work or school. Most bicycle owners in time learn to do their own running repairs, and it is not a drain on their earnings.

In the village marketplaces throughout Europe, there is always a ready sale for secondhand bicycles, which are eagerly snapped up at bargain prices by youngsters wanting their first bike. They seem to enjoy spending all their spare time on weekends tinkering with secondhand bicycles, either to use themselves or to sell.

When President Nixon visited the People's Republic of China in 1972, many reporters remarked about the lack of

In the 1970's, an English mailman still delivers his parcels on a bicycle.

An English village market scene in 1972, where bicycles are bought at bargain prices.

cars and the enormous number of bicycles on the roads. The "people's car," always the dream of the Nazi dictator of Germany, Adolf Hitler, seems to be a long way from being available in the Communist countries, but the bicycle trade flourishes. Even in Japan, a prosperous nation since World War II and one that is well ahead in the fields of electronics and ultramodern devices, nothing incongruous is seen about the mass of people using bicycles as their regular means of transport.

An important development took place in Asia in 1880 with the invention of the jinrikisha, a two-wheeled vehicle usually pulled by a single runner. The use of this vehicle spread rapidly, and for many near-starving coolies, or native laborers, the jinrikisha became the only means of earning a living. In the 1930's it began to lose its popularity and, by the beginning of World War II, was comparatively rare. However, another means of locomotion became extremely popular in the East after 1918 and that was the bicycle. Japanese companies became adept at turning them out. In many cases, the old jinrikishas that remained were converted into vehicles drawn by a man mounted on a bicycle. No one mentions coolie labor today, but jinrikishas are still used in the Far East, and probably will be as long as the cities there have so many narrow streets that are inaccessible to cars.

CHAPTER TEN

SKYCYCLING

Today one of the most popular ways to get from one place to another is by airplane. In fact, to people under twenty it must seem as if planes have always been around. Yet it was only seventy years ago that two bicycle mechanics devised the first practical "air machine." Since then millions of people have experienced man's dream of being able to soar in the skies like a bird. But that is not enough. Right now numerous experiments are going on all over the world as men try to fly planes on muscle power alone—and on bicycle energy.

For untold centuries, would-be birdmen tied on wings and jumped from high places, flapping their way into oblivion. Ironically enough, in this Space Age, when men have been to the moon and back, the dream of man *himself* flying is once again with us. The energy is supplied by pedal power, and 1971 was a great year for literally getting off the ground: bicycles began to fly!

It all began in England, the country that was responsible for the evolution of the bicycle. Two promising aircraft of this type, the Toucan and the Weybridge, were evolved, and the latter made a successful maiden flight in September of 1971. A third plane, called the Liverpuffin, was then readied for flight.

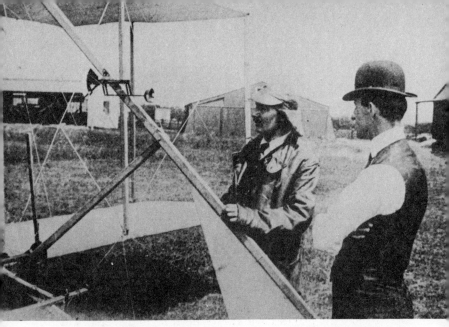

These two bicycle mechanics, Orville and Wilbur Wright, revolutionized transport throughout the world.

In Japan at the end of 1971, two new man-powered aircraft, Linnet III and Sato-Maeda OX-1, were flying. And in Canada, the Ottawa, a "skycycle" made for two, is being developed.

Interest in pedal-propelled aircraft is very high among students in the United States. The first American muscle-powered plane was the McAvoy, constructed at Georgia Tech several years ago. It was damaged before it could fly, but James M. McAvoy, Jr. of Atlanta intends to rebuild it.

Man-powered aircraft developers are very secretive about their work. Perhaps it is because flying by muscle has had a bad name ever since Icarus cracked up in Crete, but the most likely reason is that there is a $24,000 prize ready to be won by the first plane to fly a prescribed figure-eight course. Also, enthusiastic inventors probably get tired of hearing people tell them they are attempting the impossible. Everything that

has ever been invented in the past, including the original bicycle, has had to go through this phase.

By 1930 the glider, bicycle, and airplane had all been invented, and man began to put the three together to create a
flying machine he could propel by pedaling. However, studies
show that a man pedaling is capable of generating barely
enough power to sustain a very light and efficient aircraft in
an extremely brief flight. Nothing is a greater challenge to the
inventive curiosity and technical genius of man than to find
that something is almost impossible.

We have already had our pioneers in the realm of pedal-
powered planes. Flights were made in Germany and Italy
some thirty-six years ago. In these flights, the plane was not
required to take off by muscle power alone. Instead it was
catapulted into the air by stretched rubber cables that acted
as shock cords. Yet all the technology of the Germans during
the Nazi regime could produce only a plane and a sky cyclist
to range for 550 yards. A Herr Duennbeill tried to go farther
and failed, but was awarded the Reich Leader of Air Sport
prize as a compensation, a sort of Brownie point for trying.

After the war many exotic machines were built, and many
proved abortive. Renewed interest came in 1959, when the
Royal Aeronautic Society of England announced the $15,000
Kramer Competition financed by Henry Kramer, a London
industrialist. Two years after the prize was instituted, two
man-powered planes, the Southampton SUMPAC and the Hat-
field Puffin, had been built and successfully flown, taking off
and flying on unassisted muscle power. The Puffin I, flown
by John Wimpenny, set the long-distance record on May 2,
1962, by managing 993 yards. SUMPAC managed about 650
yards. They both ended their careers by crashing before they
could attend the specified course set down in the rules of the
Kramer Competition. In March 1967 Henry Kramer raised the

TOUCAN
Wingspan 123 feet
Wt. (est.) 145 lbs.

OTTAWA
Wingspan 90 feet
Wt. (est.) 209 lbs.

contest money to $24,000 and also opened it up for international competition. The prize is still waiting.

Studies show that a first-class professional cyclist *could* deliver the muscle power needed, approximately one-quarter horsepower, and get a machine such as the Puffin off the ground for ten minutes at a cruising speed of eighteen miles per hour. But it would take a superb athlete to do this. When the Puffin made its record flight, the pilot landed in a state of exhaustion.

In 1961 a fifty-nine-year-old draftsman, Bob Martyn of Calgary, Alberta, Canada, astounded his friends by building an airplane out of wood, glue, and shingle nails. People were even more surprised when it flew. Now Martyn is building a skycycle. In its experimental stages, it has wings made out of mahogany, spruce, and aluminum attached to a renovated bicycle. The pilot turns the propeller and powers the plane by pedaling away on the bicycle. Despite the fact that a well-trained bicyclist could not pedal Martyn's skycycle off the ground, the designer is not discouraged. After all, little more than a decade ago people told him that his homemade plane would never fly and he knows that it did! In eight years, he logged four-hundred flying hours in it. Martyn believes he has produced a better-designed plane than the Japanese, who have made good use of their traditional kite-making techniques.

The control panel on Martyn's man-powered plane is almost as simple as its propeller system, which works directly in relation to the turning wheels on the bicycle. A lever on the

The Toucan, built at Hertford, England, and the Ottawa, built in Canada.

left handlebar manipulates the ailerons, which create lift for the wings. Another lever, on the right handlebar, controls the rudder for direction. The trick will be to control the pilot's body motion because even a minor jerking of the head could affect the pedal plane. Those of you who bicycle will know how difficult it is simply to move the pedals around and not let something of the movement permeate the other parts of the body. But Martyn will no doubt find a way to get over this major hurdle.

Martyn's ambition is to go after the Kramer prize by pulling off a lengthy flight at an altitude greater than ten feet. Martyn says, "The Wright brothers' idea was to do their learnings at low altitudes, and I intend to do the same." This may well provide the key that will enable his pedal plane to compete for the Kramer prize.

The ideal pedal plane must have a very long wingspan and be extremely lightweight as well as aerodynamically efficient. Puffin weighed only 136 pounds and was constructed of bales covered with a featherweight material like Saran Wrap. It had a 93-foot wingspan, but it was sensitive to air gusts and could never fly in winds exceeding four miles an hour.

Apart from an expert cyclist-cum-pilot, the muscle-powered plane also seems to require a special type of sports bicycle. Students at California's Northrop Institute of Technology are building the Flycycle, a two-man pedal plane that they hope will be the first man-powered craft to fly in the United States. It will have only an eighty-foot wingspan, which seems to be a direct contradiction of the original idea that pedal planes must have an enormous wingspan. Time will tell how successful the Flycycle will be, but the idea of skycycling as a sport is something to look forward to in a world that seems to have done everything, leaving little to challenge the ingenuity of future men.

By 1971 ten muscle-powered planes had already been

flown successfully: five in Japan (Linnet I, II, III, and IV, and Sato-Maeda OX-1), four in England (SUMPAC, Puffin I, Puffin II, and Weybridge), and one in Austria, the Malliga (about which little is known). The United States was slow in producing bicycles and now seems to be slow about pedal-powered planes. However, with the technological know-how in this country, it is likely that the slow starter will beat the rest of the world if the California students continue with their enthusiastic building of the Flycycle.

The Royal Air Force in England has been secretly and seriously interested in man-powered flight for some time. In late June of 1972 the effort of some ten thousand man-hours of work was rewarded when Flight Lieutenant John Potter shattered the ten-year-old record for man-powered aircraft. He flew his pedal-powered machine for 1,171 yards at the RAF's Benson Air Station in Oxfordshire. With this flight, he managed to add another 200 yards to the existing record.

Potter says he has flown 1,200 yards before, but it did not classify for the world record. To gain status for a world record, it is necessary to have scrutineers, senior RAF officers and observers, and they have to make some stringent checks, such as measuring the area of flight.

The RAF lieutenant is an ex-Hunter fighter pilot, but his balsa-wood-and-plastic aircraft called Jupiter is the pride of his life. With it he does not have to be concerned with speed. He says that the whole flight pattern of his pedal-powered plane is far more finely tuned than the more powerful Hunter. The optimum height of Jupiter is twenty-five feet. Potter knows that edging above that altitude could make the craft stall. The Jupiter's cruise speed is 21 miles per hour, producing 0.48 horsepower. Above 25 miles per hour, the pilot's endurance is endangered by the excess effort of pedaling. Going too far below this speed brings a higher risk of stalling.

Jupiter's flights must be made on runways because the

"pedal pilot" needs a firm surface on which to start his takeoff run. Also, he needs a center line to concentrate on through his windscreen when in flight.

The Jupiter is delicate, with a wingspan of eighty feet, only four feet less than the fabulous Concorde supersonic jet, yet the total empty weight is only 146 pounds. Every wing rib took eight hours to make, and there are hundreds of them. The tailpiece has twelve thousand individually cut and glued pieces of balsa wood in it. If the skycycle had been made commercially, it would have cost about a hundred thousand dollars to build!

Ailerons are any one of certain movable plane surfaces fixed to the main planes of an air machine. They are used as balancing flaps and give stability when actuated by suitable leverage. Ailerons become effective on the pedal plane at five knots; at eight knots the rudder comes in. Slight rudder right must be used to prevent torque (a type of whiplash) from the human engine. At sixteen knots, the tail lifts; after twenty seconds, the takeoff speed of eighteen knots is reached. The pilot then has to climb twenty-five feet, and that calls for a delicate touch on the elevators. In level flight, only one artificial aid is available on the Jupiter. Should the nose of the skycycle go one degree too high or low, a light flashes on. When the skycycle comes in for touchdown, the rudder must be used to yaw the vehicle straight, otherwise the main wheel is likely to buckle.

The pilot of a skycycle has to pedal like mad to get air speed and must certainly be in the peak of physical condition. At the same time, he has to be alert enough to concentrate on making fine adjustments to the controls. Astronauts have always been considered the supermen of the air, but the skycyclist does not have a back-up of electronics to help him eliminate mistakes. It must be a most challenging experience

—to supply your own power to provide the energy to lift the skycycle into the air and then make a safe landing.

The track history of skycyclists is not too impressive, although their ambitions and desires are commendable. One of the first muscle-power men was a Bavarian tailor, L. A. Bellringer. He crashed into the Danube River in 1811.

Flight Lieutenant Potter is convinced he can do the magic mile, but to win the Kramer contest and its prize he also has to do the figure-eight course—and Jupiter's turning capacity is low. Like all young men who have the urge to fly, Potter is also optimistic that in time he can conquer the difficulty of maneuverability. It would be unsportsmanlike to think that Kramer put in the figure-eight course to keep his money safe!

The great fear of any skycyclist must always be concern with what can happen even in a minor crash. The skycycles are so delicately made that any small diversion from the norm could result in a tragedy. Perhaps that only adds to the interest in skycycling.

Unless the students in California come up with something truly spectacular, it is likely that British inventors will take the lead in skycycling, just as they led in the evolution and development of the basic bicycle. John Wimpenny of St. Albans is regarded as the father of successful pedal pilots, and John Potter is carrying on in the same tradition. The reason for the interest of the Royal Air Force is clear. There is likely to be some strong competition from the Russians, who are working on a skycycle that will hover and fly sideways. If the RAF can beat the Russian team and be the first to capture the Kramer prize, it would be a prestigious national victory.

The Kramer Competition to date has been too tough for anyone to tackle, but the Flycycle of California and the Canadian pedal planes are the most likely ones to rival the Jupiter on the seemingly impossible course. The contestants will need that certain splendid type of madness that we call genius. There are so few new worlds to conquer that the last transportation frontier may well be the bicycle that flies—the pedal-powered plane.

DIALOGUE OF THE FUTURE:

"Look! Up there in the sky!"
"It's a bird!"
"It's a plane!"
"It's Superman!"
"No, dear—it's just a flying bicycle."

CHAPTER ELEVEN

THE BICYCLE AND YOU

In the last five years or so, we have seen the bicycle being rediscovered by many Americans. It started as a fad; now it has become a cult, an expression of freedom by young people seeking a new awareness on all levels of life. But we should not think that only the young are interested in bicycling. Older people are aware of its health-giving qualities too.

In the 1972 Presidential election year, the bicycle was very much a part of the hullabaloo that goes with politics in the United States, although it did not quite outdo the fashion of hitchhiking, which young Americans have brought to a fine art both in this country and in Europe when on vacation. On June 17, seven bicyclists left Avon, Senator George McGovern's childhood home in South Dakota. Their target was the site of the Democratic convention in Miami Beach, a distance of seventeen hundred miles. They sold campaign and peace buttons all along their route to pay their expenses and arrived in time for the convention, complete with bicycle decals saying "We Want McGovern" and, perhaps just as important, other, larger decals stating "This vehicle is smog free."

Of course, other bicyclists attended the convention, but the seven from Avon captured more attention because of the length of their journey on bicycles. One of the cyclists, Fred Karlin, pointed out that his marathon riding group included,

Cycling has never known any age limits.

Courtesy Montagu Motor Museum, Beaulieu, Hants., England

besides black and white Americans, two native American Indian women and a Mexican American, with ages ranging from seventeen to thirty-one. The seven riders were in good physical condition when they arrived, and everyone admitted it was an experience they had enjoyed and would not have missed for anything. This seems to prove that with goodwill and a bicycle, the world is an oyster that can be opened wide, bringing a sense of pleasurable achievement to those who neither want nor need an automobile.

The Boy Scout Association, known all over the world, offers a merit badge for bicycling, and training for this badge means learning road manners and safety rules. More and more Boy Scouts are going in for this merit badge. Side by side with it, some schools now ask members of their local police force to give their time on a voluntary basis to instruct young people on how to ride a bicycle safely.

The United States is a great place for club activities. There are clubs for just about everything, so it is inevitable that groups of people in quite small communities are gathering together to form their own bicycling clubs. After that, they begin to organize trail rides, and young people are able to see more of their own country and to feel a greater affinity with nature. Our grandparents did it, and now we are doing the same. The more we see and understand our own countryside, even if it is only a few miles away from home, the less we are likely to want to defile and pollute it. Recently we have noticed groups of bicyclists riding along or stopping to admire views or just to rest, and we have been conscious that they rarely leave litter behind.

A cyclist can go seven times as far as he could on his own two feet and not use up any more energy. It's like having a legendary pair of seven-league boots and, in addition to the pleasure and practicality of bicycling, there is a bonus in the form of better health.

Bicycling can be the antidote for work strain and for the tensions caused by the fast-moving age in which we live. Bicycling provides a change of pace, scenery, and action, and also acts in such a way on the body, mind, and spirit that energy and enthusiasm are rekindled.

Many of our everyday jobs, whether at school, at work, or at home, do not require us to use our muscles. Bicycling, however, solves that problem. It is rhythmic and helps to get the blood circulating. One of the best things about it is that practically anyone can do it; age and health have only little significance. In fact, nonmoving bicycles have been used in hospital therapy, especially in the United States, for such things as broken legs, ankles, and feet. Fractured limbs will respond to the gentle massaging effect of pedaling, and it helps relax the muscles in general.

Once you are used to it, it is possible to cycle fifty miles a day regularly, but if there is a break in this pattern, you will have to start all over again with a ten-mile ride, increasing the distance a little every day. Ten to fifteen miles a day is usually a good distance for beginners to aim at.

The same rule applies in racing. It is better to go in for the short-distance races and build up to the marathons or great cross-country races. Unless you are sure you are in good condition, it is better not to race all-out. Naturally, it is exhilarating to win a twenty-five-mile race, but you will have a lot of fun merely taking part in it. We have yet to meet a racing bicyclist who came in last who did not say that he enjoyed his ride.

Pacing is also necessary for the person who wants to use

The lightweight Carlton, a finely constructed bicycle for the professional rider.

Members of the Missileland Wheels Cycling Club of Florida. This kind of scene is becoming increasingly common in towns throughout the United States.

Courtesy of The Orlando Sentinel

his bicycle for touring. Work out a route and take time to consider any specific scenic views or historic sites that you may want to visit. But be flexible in your riding schedule, because a head wind can slow down even a good, trained bicyclist. A normal day's ride could be sixty miles, with little pressure on the rider, but you should always take time to stop for meals, conversation, appreciation of the countryside, and visits to landmarks. You can also indulge in other hobbies, such as photography, mapmaking, and archaeology, while on a tour.

Built in the finest tradition of English design and craftsmanship, this custom-made cycle by Bob Jackson must have a place in the annals of great bicycles. It is a single-geared 14½-pound track-racing bicycle, traditionally sold without brakes.

The elegant Chopper, made by Raleigh.

Often, though, when young people go camping on a tour of several days' duration, they are inclined to take too much with them. Maybe that is a result of those family camping tours by automobile when it seems imperative to take all the joys of home life along, including the kitchen stove.

Bicycling should not be reduced to being just a challenge to go faster than anyone else or to cover more miles. Every minute on the vehicle should be pleasurable. There is even a rare sense of achievement in feeling tired at the end of a day's ride, and you will be storing up memories to talk about in the future.

A person should start cycling when he is young and continue as he gets older. This is really all the training that is needed—unless one wants to go in for racing. Anyone who is fit is less prone to get sick, especially to catch colds and the flu—even the more exotic forms of this strange virus. Exposure to the open air combined with exercise can ward off the many chills and coughs that so many people accept as part of their lives. Outdoor exercise should become a lifelong habit. The more oxygen we get into our blood system, the better we feel; we also become more alert and can cope with such things as school examinations with little tension and strain.

In the early stages of enthusiasm, girls probably take to bicycling more easily than boys. They are more inclined to develop specific styles in riding and are less obsessed with speed. In races, women can hold their own with men despite

The tricycle is making a comeback in the Space Age.

the fact that their hearts and lungs are often smaller. Women can be cunning race riders, capable of outmaneuvering the opposite sex.

Today we face a steadily worsening transportation crisis, and nothing that can alleviate it should be ignored. The bicycle can play an important role in people's lives as a pleasure vehicle, but it also has a role to play as a means to future mobility. Everything you can do to dignify the role of the bicyclist and to help others who are interested in cycling will ultimately make politicians realize that the bicycle is more than a fad—it is a way to solve many of our current problems.

If you are interested in conservation and want a better environment, then you should know that bicycles are part of the answer. They represent a challenge to the automobile with its noise and unhealthy exhaust fumes, its need for ever more strips of concrete across the land, and its burden on personal finances. Bicycles offer instead an alternate means of mobility that is quiet, clean, healthy, space saving, and economical.

Modern bicycle designers have kept faith with the early designers by updating models, but the next move is to get the politicians to *think cycleways!*

INDEX